THE ATONEMENT AND THE SOCIAL PROCESS

OTHER BOOKS BY

SHAILER MATHEWS

Selected Mediæval Documents
The French Revolution, 1789-1815
A History of New Testament Times in Palestine
The Spiritual Interpretation of History

Patriotism and Religion
The Making of Tomorrow
The Validity of American Ideals

Jesus on Social Institutions
The Social Gospel
The Individual and the Social Gospel
The Church and the Changing Order
The Gospel and the Modern Man
The Faith of Modernism
The Messianic Hope in the New Testament
Contributions of Science to Religion
(with 13 scientists)
A Constructive Life of Christ
(with E. D. Burton)
A Dictionary of Religion and Ethics
(with G. B. Smith)
The Student's Gospels
(with E. J. Goodspeed)

THE ATONEMENT AND THE SOCIAL PROCESS

BY

SHAILER MATHEWS

DEAN OF THE DIVINITY SCHOOL OF THE UNIVERSITY OF CHICAGO

NEW YORK

THE MACMILLAN COMPANY

1930

Set up and electrotyped.

SET UP BY BROWN BROTHERS LINOTYPERS
PRINTED IN THE UNITED STATES OF AMERICA
BY THE FERRIS PRINTING COMPANY

CONTENTS

CHAPTER		PAGE
I.	The Social Origin of Christian Doctrines	9
II.	Christian Doctrines as Social Patterns .	30
III.	The Death of Christ Interpreted in the Messianic Pattern	40
IV.	The Death of Christ in the Pattern of Sacrifice	49
V.	The Death of Christ in the Pattern of Acquittal	61
VI.	The Death of Christ Interpreted in the Pattern of Sonship	79
VII.	The Rise of the Imperial Pattern in Western Christianity	89
VIII.	The Death of Christ in the Pattern of Feudalism	99
IX.	The Death of Christ in the Pattern of Monarchy	115
X.	Modifications of the Political Pattern .	143
XI.	The Functional Value of the Doctrines of the Atonement	164
XII.	The Death of Christ in the Pattern of Process	177
	Index	211

THE ATONEMENT AND THE SOCIAL PROCESS

THE ATONEMENT AND THE SOCIAL PROCESS

CHAPTER I

THE SOCIAL ORIGIN OF CHRISTIAN DOCTRINES

RELIGIONS, like men, have their days of judgment when they are tried for their lives. Not alone in Greece has been heard the wail, "Great Pan is dead." Few religions have been able to withstand radical changes in the structure of society. Humanity is pragmatic. While ancient beliefs may be honored as bric-a-brac, they are not likely to be given intellectual respect, for when a religion ceases to be intellectually respectable it is senile.

It is true that the case of religion is often tried before some revolutionary tribunal more eager to condemn than to acquit. But such tribunals are seldom permanent. The really critical moment for a religion is when it is challenged by a new social mind to give reasons for its existence. Such moments come when a social order becomes so complicated that the old authorities and customs no longer furnish unquestioned moral guidance. The supreme issue is not forced by science alone. Scientific method is not necessarily the enemy of religious faith for, whether consciously or not, it presupposes faith in working hypotheses rather than absolute knowledge. The severest test to which religion can be subjected is that set by the mind-set of social groups. Into such mind-sets a great variety of elements enter. Men accept or reject religious practices and doctrines for no very clear reasons, often because of some unconscious affinity or enmity. A religion either does or does not meet the needs of which men are aware. One does not need to be a philosopher to share in the mind-set served by philosophy any more than he needs to be a musician to prefer Beethoven to jazz. But a religion, let it be repeated, must be intellectually respectable if it is to win permanent standing in a social order.

Yet intellectual respectability is not first, but second in point of time when compared with religious life itself. The attitudes that are embodied in a religious group can be shared by those who have abandoned the reasons by which the attitudes are justified. They will themselves furnish their own reasons when the need of reasons is felt.

I

The history of Christianity is one phase of general history. In particular it involves the development of the Christian movement from its origins to the present condition, not as something apart from the development of civilization, but as one aspect thereof. Any study of

Christianity must take into account the development of the social process which gave rise to the situations in which doctrines were developed. To some extent this has been recognized by the historians of doctrines, but too often only in an encyclopedic fashion. Instead of treating Christianity as a continuous group movement of people possessed of a common loyalty to Jesus, they seem to regard it more as a system existing apart from people. The effect of such a preconception is to center attention on doctrine and to make the great question for the theologian the truthfulness of any doctrine. This in turn leads to a discussion of the validity of the authority upon which the doctrine has been built.

Such a method ignores the fact that doctrines have not sprung up as independent systems of truth. In this respect they do not resemble philosophy so much as statutory law and especially the common law of England and the Constitution of the United States. In order to understand a doctrine one must know not only the time and place of its formulation, but also the social and religious tensions which gave rise to it. Strictly speaking, there is no history of doctrine; there is only the history of the people who made doctrines. A theology is a function of the religious life of a given period and this in turn is the expression of a social order conditioned not only by elements of culture, like philosophy, literature, and science, but also by the creative economic and political forces which engage in the production of the social order itself. One can understand the history of Christianity only as a social eddy within the main current of the stream of history. It may become an object of special investigation, but only as it is a phase of the social history.

When a group is aware of a tension between its religious heritage and the new conditions under which it must live, its method of procedure is likely to be one or more of the following:

It may endeavor to crush the new conditions; it may abandon its inheritances; it may undertake to evaluate and reëxpress its inheritances; it may undertake to find some pattern in which the new and the old can be combined.

The rise of theologies cannot be understood if this adjustment of tensions is neglected. The full purport of a doctrine cannot be seen until it is regarded in the light of its origins as a means of legitimatizing some element of the precious religious heritage which the group organizing the doctrine wishes to preserve.

From such point of view the test of any doctrine is not absolute, but pragmatic—that is to say, its capacity to vindicate the deepest faith and the moral conduct of that group of Christians by which it was drawn up. If a doctrine is to be appreciated it is necessary to study historically the origin of the spiritual tension from which it sprang. Therein are the reasons for its existence In such case it may very likely be that a doctrine relieved a tension and legitimatized a belief which were themselves unwarranted. For example, one needs only to mention the various doctrines dealing with hell and the devil. In each case some doctrine made the acceptance of irrational beliefs tenable for the people subject to the tension.

Whoever would understand a doctrine, however, and evaluate it as an element in our modern religious life, must do something more than understand its origin and function. These are preliminary to a discussion as to whether any such tension now exists and if the doctrine historically developed meets a new tension which has resulted from the passage of Christian life and thought into a different world from that in which the doctrine was needed and developed. For religious experience is more permanent than its intellectual vindication.

It is at this point that one sees the importance of discovering what the real nature of doctrines is. In every case, with the possible exception of consubstantiability, the doctrines in Christianity are not metaphysical. They are patterns derived from that total social life with which it is the business of the church historian to become acquainted. For it is the influence of the social forces in the midst of which the churches lived that shaped the pattern which relieved the tension and, indeed, may have caused the tension itself.

As one approaches theology, therefore, from the historical point of view it is desirable not only to gauge religious needs but also to watch the pattern-making process, both from the point of view of the tension and from the point of view of its adjustment. Each study is indispensable. Religious experience is antecedent to doctrines and both can be understood accurately only as they are related to a culture.

II

It is not uncommon to confuse theology with a philosophy or a philosophy of religion. But when one actually asks not what theology might be or ought to be, but what it actually is, it is clear enough that it is very different from a philosophy. Theology was born of the association of men possessed of a common loyalty, from which emerged the organization of a group belief; a philosophy is not dependent upon elements due to association but is accepted or rejected by individuals as such.[1]

The correctness of this distinction at once appears when one recalls the course of events through which various theologies have been formed. Without exception, one will find that our theologies, even when held by a professedly non-creedal group like the Baptists, are really the result of imitation, customs, discussion, conflict, compromise, and successive decisions of groups. At first these groups generally were small, but more or less rapidly joined, and expressed their already formulated beliefs in councils or assemblies or something similar. The theology, for example, of most Protestant

[1] For a discussion of the bearing of the social mind upon Christianity as a developing religion see Mathews, *The Faith of Modernism*. The results of that study are embodied in this chapter.

bodies gathers around some Confession which has been adopted by some church body. Many of these Confessions were adopted by political bodies like the Parliament of England, or by bodies expressly representing some municipal unit like the Swiss cities.

If one traces these group deliverances of Christianity back to their origin, the importance of councils and other bodies grows even more distinct. The Council of Nicea made the first attempt at formulating a belief that should be held by the churches of an empire. That its decisions and those of other ecumenical councils were accepted by the total group represented appears from the fact that genuine ecumenical dogma has never been drawn up since the division of the Roman Empire. While the Roman church regards its councils as ecumenical, such a view compels the reduction of the great Eastern churches into schismatics and Protestants into heretics.

Ecclesiastical decisions have usually been enforced by group authority rather than by argument. Church groups like all others seek self-preservation by compelling individuals to assent to group decisions. Excommunication from the church and punishment by civil authorities have both alike served to give success to orthodoxy. Whatever might have happened if circumstances had been different, the historical fact is that the decisions of successive councils, Greek, Lutheran, Calvinistic, Anglican, Presbyterian, in fact of every ecclesiastical body able to get control of the machinery of the state, owe their success over opposing groups or individuals to coercion.

Looking now still more closely at the history of this fact, it becomes apparent that those doctrines became permanent which were held by the dominant political and social group. Heresy is always the belief of a defeated party. If it had succeeded it would have been orthodoxy. A striking illustration of this fact is the history of the Nicene formula during the reigns of the various Roman emperors. Arian and Athanasian doctrines were successively authoritative. But those groups who held the Athanasian views finally got control of state and church. The success of later bodies which gave permanent organization to Christian teaching always lay with those who could enforce their decisions. From the exclusively historical point of view, the issue between groups holding opposing views was not so much one of truth as of ability to enforce a decision. Personally, I think that in general the decisions reached by the formers of orthodoxy were nearer the truth than the views proposed by heretics, but history is not a normative but a descriptive science.

At this point a fact of importance appears: Latin and Protestant theology is composed of the doctrines which were held by those social groups who evolved and organized Western civilization. Orthodoxy may be described as the doctrine which satisfied the needs of the more creative and constructive minds. Our Western civilization and Western theology have the same line of social ancestry. The social psychology of the one is the social psychology of the other. Both are the product of the stronger rather than the weaker group life. So far is it from being true that Christianity is a plea for "defeatism."

III

These facts so baldly stated become a point of departure not only for the interpretation of the religious development of an evolving social order, but also for the specific doctrines as to the significance of the death of Jesus. Such doctrines, when arranged according to their origin chronologically, synchronize with the creative epochs of European history. They embody the dominant characteristics and practices of the period in which they were finally organized.

In this regard they illustrate the entire development of Western Christianity as the religious aspect of Western civilization.

Western civilization has passed through several distinguishable stages. Each of these produced one or more of the great doctrines of orthodoxy.

1. The Græco-Roman world was non-political and little interested in social reform. It had noble philosophies which might have resulted in distinct social advance and an intelligent reform of fatal economical conditions, but all such influence was estopped by the fact that the Græco-Roman world was under the control of a foreign power. It was not creative, it was

reflective and critical. The great period of social and political construction had already passed when Alexander died. From that day to this, the Near East has been a liability which the Western world has repeatedly tried to liquidate. Estopped from political and social creativeness, the Hellenistic mind turned almost passionately to philosophy and religion, developing an amazing loquacity which often passed for metaphysics and faith.

The Roman mind on the contrary was essentially practical, and its interest in metaphysical speculations was acquired and never determinative. The Western world was built up by the Romans in much the same way that America has been built up by Anglo-Saxons. Its very structure was Roman. Herein it differed markedly from the East, where the Roman administration was not creative but superimposed upon older civilizations.[2]

The break-up of the Western civilization by the armed immigration of German tribes not only destroyed the Roman population and civilization, but it forced Europe back into a condition from which feudalism emerged as a method of social reorganization. Out from the feudal world emerged the nationalist and, because of causes which it is not necessary to specify, there came later the era of the *bourgeois* democracies.

[2] Yet sovereignty concepts were present in Eastern theologies and worship. Cf. Chrysostom's exposition of the Eastern liturgy of his day.

2. All these stages in the development of Western civilization found expression in the contemporary religious life. The Hellenistic social mind gave us the doctrines of the Trinity and Christology and diverted Christianity from the moral goal set by Jesus to a theology. The primary tests of Christian loyalty were doctrinal and without explicit moral elements. The Roman social mind perpetuated this metaphysical interest but it also developed a great imperialistic church where creeds became to all intents and purposes law. Out from the collapse of this Roman creativeness came our doctrine of original sin and the sovereignty of God, as well as the Roman Catholic church, in form and genius a transcendentalized Roman Empire.

Feudal practice found expression in the Anselmic doctrine of the atonement, by which God is conceived of as a feudal lord, having an honor which must be satisfied before he is free to undertake the salvation of men whom he wishes to take the place of the fallen angels.

The rise of nations was accompanied by the rise of national churches which perpetuated practically the entire theological scheme of the imperialistic Roman church, but which conceived of God as a king, and his relations with men as subject to conditions identical with those found in the new states. It is no accident that Protestantism never succeeded within the boundaries of the old Roman Empire. Social inheritances there were too fundamentally imperialistic.

The *bourgeois* period led certain groups of Christians to emphasize the rights of man before God, just as the period itself developed the rights of man over against kings. Democracies evolved democratic churches. The Congregationalists, Baptists, and Unitarians never controlled state religions like Lutheranism, Anglicanism, and Presbyterianism, and their methods of organization were based on the competency of the individual. With them orthodoxy is an inheritance rather than a creation.

IV

Such facts as these make it impossible to believe that theology is a child of philosophy. It is far more correct to say that it is the intellectual legitimization of a life that sought religious help for its weakness, ideals for its energies, and satisfaction for its needs. The method of this legitimization is the description of the relations of men and God as identical with those which are contemporaneously creative in a social order. The patterns of theology are given by social experience. Evidence of this is in the vocabulary of theology itself. While it is true our technical theological systems have inherited certain terms which came over from Scholasticism, these terms are incidental and technical. There are only two doctrines, the vocabulary of which does not seem to have been taken from experience, namely, those of the Trinity and Christology. But a study of the development of the doctrine of the Trinity will show that the primary interest of the church of the second to the fourth century was not metaphysical but soteriological. The primitive Christians were Jews who cast the gospel in the terms of Jewish Messianism. In the course of a century the Christian church was a group of non-Jews who had accepted the unfamiliar vocabulary of the authoritative literature of the Bible but sought to reëxpress and legitimize their experience of salvation in the thought forms of philosophical monotheism. The resulting doctrine as to God was the product of the confluence of the religious experience of the Hebrew and the Greek, later affected somewhat by the imported views of the Far East. The biblical vocabulary was forced into the thought patterns of the new Christian group. "Consubstantial," obviously a metaphysical term, is the one metaphysical term of Christian theology. "Persona," derived from the law courts, gained metaphysical significance when the Greeks endeavored to give such a quality to a striking metaphor of Tertullian. And even then, as has already been pointed out, such metaphysical interest was a phase of the Græco-Roman social mind.

Other than the term "consubstantial," however, the vocabulary of historical orthodoxy is that of social experience. The tri-personal God issues "decrees" and publishes "law." He "punishes" those who violate the law and prepares a blessed future for those who observe it. Man's inability to keep the law results from a definite act of "disobedience" on the part of Adam who propagated sin and corruption among his descendants of whom he becomes a "representative." God "elects" certain of the members of this "guilty" race to be saved and his right to "forgive" is justified by various conceptions of the atonement, all of which introduce the death of Christ into a transcendentalized penology current in the time the doctrine is made (as, for example, the ransom, the satisfaction of the divine honor, the satisfaction of punitive justice, the payment of a debt, the vindication of the sovereignty of the law). Those who are thus elected and forgiven are said to be justified or "acquitted." The completion of the saving process is the establishment of the Kingdom of God.

These terms are not philosophical; almost exclusively they are juridical or political. Our theology can best be described as a transcendentalized politics reproducing the group custom and institutions which have appeared in Western civilization. Vocabularies were furnished by the social patterns into which religious thought was put.

But the origin of a term is less important than its use. In the history of Christianity, an experience has preceded its explanation and definition. The first group of Christians had no theology, but they had a loyalty and a hope. This in itself was quasi-political, namely, that Jesus was to establish the kingdom of David in accordance with the current messianic hope, itself political. But this common attitude of individuals, which drew them together into a group, soon by the inevitable laws of group life demanded a vocabulary, and thus from the start words came to be the expression and symbol of the group attitude. The Christians are those of the *Way*, *Nazarenes*, the *disciples of Jesus*, and finally *Christians*. The next step was to give unity to this group life and to distinguish it from others by the gradual choice of certain words as tests. They were not severely scientific; one might almost say they were sacramental, the outward symbol of an inward meaning. Thus to call Jesus "Lord" was to express the fundamental group attitude of loyalty and hope in him, but New Testament scholarship finds it hard to agree on any definition of the title.

Similarly with other terms. As the Christian movement extended and groups became geographically scattered, there came inevitably the effort to organize a common group attitude into a characteristic group belief by means of standardized terms. The first step was taken by relatively small and scattered groups through discussion and discipline. But discussion became widespread. What term could properly express the common group belief? Should it be the term "Logos," or the term "Christ," or the term "the Son of God"; if all three, in what sense could these be used? By the middle of the second century, Christian groups began to use terms in a somewhat different sense, rival groups insisting that their views were correct. For a couple of centuries discussion continued, different groups using different terms or the same words according to their own custom and fixing such usage by group action in synods and councils. Strictly speaking, these groups never arrived at an exact definition of the terms they used (compare the creed of Chalcedon), but in the long process of controversy, terms came to correlate different attitudes. Thus the word *homoousios* (of the same substance) indicated one fundamental type of religious attitude and *homoiousios* (of a like substance) another. It is not strange that groups characterized by the one or the other could not express their positions with thorough intelligibility, yet make each term a rallying point and banner of a party. When the party of *homoousia* fortunately won, it was natural that its term should be authoritative; but even a cursory knowledge of the history of post-Nicene theology shows that the word was reinterpreted and redescribed, until its real content as given by the Cappadocians was different from that given it by Athanasius. Yet it served as a legitimate symbol of a group attitude and a group belief as to Jesus, beyond question more consistent with religious efficiency and reasonableness than were those symbolized by the other term. This attitude and this loyalty were definitely built into the Christian movement by the use of social patterns.

Similarly in the case of other terms. They were all chosen first as striking analogies or patterns, as a means of clarifying group belief. That which was accepted as a matter of course in social experience was used to describe the relation of God and man. Terms with their new connotation became by custom the symbols of parties rather than the exact embodiment of truth.

The impatience which theological reformers show with all inherited terms is a tribute to their neglect of the laws of social psychology. Our theology is not a system of philosophy, but an extension of the forms of social experience to religious belief. It is a sort of parable in whose plot can be read the history of the social experience of centuries. Its purpose is to make religious experience consistent with other experience, and so reasonable. In failing to pay full respect to this social value of pattern-terms, theological reformers are in danger of denying the religious values which patterns embody.

V

The social origin of doctrines is also seen in the fact that many of them are the outcome of religious customs and practices of groups. How else can one account for the doctrines of the mass, baptismal regeneration, transubstantiation, Sabbath observance, the worship of saints, the use of images, the infallibility of the Pope speaking *ex cathedra*? In all these cases customs grew up, became characteristic of groups and then of larger groups, until they became so common, significant, and sacred as to be constituent elements in religion itself. To remove them was impossible except by revolution. Rather than to face such a crisis Christian groups have explained them, made them into doctrines, and enforced them with authority. Indeed, the chief difference between various Christian groups is precisely in the field of doctrines which originated in, preserve, and systematize customs.

VI

The practical value of these facts is considerable, and may be stated as a group of corollaries.

1. Theology is functional. The Christians of each period inherited the beliefs of their predecessors. In so far as this heritage failed to satisfy new needs, they reëxamined it and found in it values which were capable of explication and restatement in new social conditions and with new social patterns.

Two conclusions follow from this fact. First, members of groups governed by the same loyalties and values can, if they choose, use the same terms with differently defined content. This situation will probably be only temporary, but it is frequent. A term like "Son of God," for instance, has had a variety of definitions and usages, ranging from "Messiah" to "Second Person" in a metaphysical Trinity. But its religious value or symbolism when applied to Jesus has been constant. It has expressed the conviction that through Jesus God has been uniquely revealed. If theology were a science composed of accurate definitions, it would be necessary that all parties use the term with exactly the same understanding and content. But this is impossible and has never occurred. The flag of a country has the same meaning to patriots no matter of what material it is composed, and a theology is the symbol, the banner of a common group attitude and not a mass of definitions given identical content by all members of the group.

Second, a term that no longer expresses a religious value or serves as the symbol of a group attitude should be abandoned. As a matter of fact, this generally happens in current religious discussions. Confessional theology perpetuates a vocabulary which became necessary to some system, but which may mean nothing to the religious life of to-day. The reason for this is plain. It no longer connotes or symbolizes the essential attitude or loyalty.

2. If theology is functional, the same Christian attitudes and loyalties have been and still can be represented by different terms and formulas. This is evident in such words as "Christ," "Son of God," "Savior," "Lord." But it is equally true of other terms, especially those interpreting the death of Jesus. The common divisor of Christian groups is their attitude toward God as revealed in and by Jesus. The theological patterns will vary.

Social interests are bound to develop some form of theology to-day as hitherto, but these interests may not be the same as in the past. In the place of an autocratic king, we have democracy. It is not possible for a man thoroughly in sympathy with modern tendencies to use the formulas of our inherited thology with satisfaction. He knows that the conception of a king which is reflected in the theological doctrine of the sovereignty of God is outgrown. Yet the conception of God as the ultimate reality with whom men must accord, survives. We may well expect to see this expressed in theological conceptions drawn from our democratic experience. In fact, we already are beginning to use terms which make our inherited faith in God more vital and effective. As over against the old conception of royal sovereignty external to and not dependent upon the nation, we have the conception of sovereignty immanent in the nation itself, but transcendental to that nation when expressing itself in governmental forms. In the case of American law, government with sovereignty expressed in the judicial, legislative, and executive elements, might even serve as a pattern for the Trinity. Our group experience, through free discussion, will find an analogy which will express the profound religious conviction that while God is immanent in nature he also must be thought of as expressing himself objectively to that nature, especially to humanity. The process of making this theology does not involve transformation of values and attitudes which older theologies expressed for their authors, but rather the discovery of certain social practices and experiences, which as patterns will actually and constructively express our religious loyalties and beliefs. Theology will change but Christian experience and faith embodied in the Christian movement will continue. If prophecy be in any way justified, it would seem certain that the values which have been carried along through the evangelical theologies are those which are to persist. Just as certain economic presuppositions have emerged from the storm and stress of the economic life of the past, and in different expositions stand tested by their satisfaction of humanity's needs, so the great values which have been increasingly realized and expressed by successive theologies, reflecting successive social experiences, will continue to project themselves into the religious life of the future. They will give rise to new doctrines as group interests change, but Christianity will breed true to itself because it will be developed by groups of Christians whose needs and satisfactions are of the same general type. Social psychology is as inevitable as society. New social needs will give rise to new religious needs, patterns, and formulas, just as they develop new laws and governments. New occasions will not only teach new duties, but they will also teach new patterns in which to set forth the consistency of the realities of the spirit with those other realities which go to make up our world. Discussion by which new formulas for old values are shaped will be feared only by those who wish to maintain social or ecclesiastical privilege.

CHAPTER II

CHRISTIAN DOCTRINES AS SOCIAL PATTERNS

A BELIEF gets theological or philosophical value only when interpreted. Such interpretation it is that distinguishes the history of thought from encyclopedic information. To be understood a fact must be identified with some unquestioned conception or social practice. When one is convinced that a fact has a bearing upon actual life the desire to rationalize such a belief leads to the discovery of some inclusive formula which connects it with that which is unquestioned. Obviously this process is a form of analogy. Some similarity is discovered between that to be interpreted and that which is a matter of common and unquestioned experience. Sometimes this analogy is frankly a comparison, as when Jesus says that the kingdom of God is like leaven; at other times it is metaphorical, as when the psalmist declares that the Lord is the rock of his salvation. In such cases the analogical quality is clearly recognized by its author. But interpretation is not content with conscious analogy. A satisfactory interpretation comes only when a description is regarded as fact rather than analogical, axiomatic rather than imagined. When the past spoke of God as a spirit or as a sovereign, when the practices of courtiers and the conceptions of the law court were employed to describe men's relations with God, such descriptions were not regarded as analogical but as elements in the religious conceptions themselves. That is to say, they were patterns rather than metaphors. For a pattern is a social institution or practice used to give content and intelligibility to otherwise unrationalized beliefs. What the axiom is to mathematics, a pattern is in thought. Later criticism may discover the analogical character of the pattern, but as long as it brings intellectual serenity and allays intellectual obscurity a pattern is regarded as fact rather than as metaphor. As such it forms a distinct element in the total conception which expresses religious fact or an element of faith.

I

All Christian doctrines are patterns. They originated in the impulse to make something intelligible by discovering a likeness to something unquestioned. But among the various metaphors so used some ceased to be used as metaphors and became realities which could be analyzed and from which corollaries could be drawn. That is, they became patterns. So long as these patterns were the projection of existing social institutions and practices they brought intellectual assent. To include any element of faith within the pattern was to give it acceptability. Its new classification with accepted reality deadened doubt and prevented intellectual irritation. Men could continue to believe and hope.

It is difficult to draw a line sharply between metaphors thus used as facts and those which were consciously analogical, yet as one reviews the past these differences are apparent. The pattern becomes basic to an interpretation and this interpretation is subject to extensive development. Thus the conception of sovereignty carries within itself such corollaries as the absolute power of the monarch, decrees, law and its violations, trials, sentences, pardon, reward, and punishment. It is in this pattern that the more highly developed interpretations of the death of Christ arose. Indeed, every doctrine of the atonement may be said to be the use of some social pattern resolving a difficulty perceived in God's forgiveness of sinners and of the death of Christ as a basis upon which this forgiveness could be justified. The difficulty and its cure alike have sprung from a social practice.

That which gives value to the pattern is the fact that men do not regard it as analogical. When its analogical quality is discovered its integrating power disappears. Most religious doubts arise when a pattern is seen to be a metaphor. The social practice or institution which has been used as a pattern no longer has meaning or social control. Yet the value that has been rationalized by a social pattern can be appreciated when the analogical nature of the doctrine itself is recognized. That is to say, theology gets its lasting value when we come to see that it is a functional rather than a final method of coördinating religious faith with accepted realities. Speaking generally, orthodox theology is the use of political experience to set forth the reasonableness of Christian confidence in salvation. It is, in fact, transcendentalized politics. But this is not to say that it is without value. It certainly helped its creators. As a method of rationalizing existing religious belief it follows the method which humanity always has pursued and endeavors to find reasonableness in the use of social pattern. It is only when, because of change of social institutions and processes, any given pattern fails to coördinate and so to give reasonableness to religious experience that criticism arises.

When such criticism appears the value that the doctrinal pattern expressed can be recovered very simply by recalling the origin of the pattern in a social practice so universal as to be unquestioned. The interpretative formula is something like this: as an absolute monarch was to his subjects, so is God to his people. The truth lies in the analogy rather than in the description of God as king. That is, God is the conditioning fact in religion. The same thing is true of other doctrines. Whatever a social institution meant to a given social situation becomes the analogical expression of a religious value.

The successive definitions given the death of Christ are striking illustrations of the pattern-making process of the Christian religion. For their authors they were the means of rationalizing Christian experience and faith. Yet when they ceased to represent creative and unquestioned social practices, they have been sources of intellectual unrest. Whatever permanent value they may express must be discovered by a study of the function of patterns from the point of view of social psychology. By such an equation we arrive at actual religious needs, and the satisfactions given by the death of Christ to Christian experience.

II

Obviously the student of a religion must be historically minded. Not truth, but fact, is the first subject of his search. Only after he has impartially described the religion is he in a position to measure its permanent values.

Such an attitude is especially demanded of a student of any religion of which he is himself a follower. If a Christian would understand Christianity he must examine its history in scientific detachment, otherwise he is apt to take apologetic short cuts to assent. He must not permit his detachment to become distrust or his individual faith to become a criterion. He must first describe if he would understand.

From the strictly historical point of view Christianity as a religion is a technique of salvation, but just what salvation is and what it is from which men are saved have been repeatedly described. No single formula has had permanent control of the Christian's hope. Jesus made love the central attitude of morality, but he had no social program and no philosophy. In the first form of Christianity, Jews, whose revolutionary psychology had been given new direction by their acceptance of Jesus as the one empowered by God's spirit to be the savior of their nation, made salvation a sublimated nationalism. But a nation's future was soon seen to be of secondary value. Men lived in a world of tragedy, and expected a new world of joy. They believed themselves the sport of Satan and his demons, but they also believed that Jesus would ultimately save them as individuals by crushing the forces of the Prince of Evil. They found themselves mortal and doomed to death, but they believed that those who had experienced the regenerating influence of the Spirit which Jesus sent from heaven would when freed from their flesh be given new bodies and made citizens of a heavenly society. They found themselves the prey of passion and evil desire, but they looked forward to the time when, freed from these, they would live according to the Spirit. They awaited an awful Judgment Day, but because of their faith in Jesus they expected to be acquitted and admitted into the joys of the new age they awaited.

This hope of salvation is very different from the philosophy of Epictetus or Marcus Aurelius. The deliverance which the first Christians awaited was to be not only supernatural but limited to those who were followers of Jesus. The world lay in wickedness; the reborn children of God had passed from death to life. They awaited neither a political reformation nor the evolution of a better social order, but an emancipating catastrophe.

These characteristics the Christian religion has never wholly lost. True, there have been those who would translate it into some philosophy or social program, but they constitute almost a negligible fraction of the hundreds of millions of people who have sought deliverance through Christ from whatever evils they endured in a present world and the imagined evils which were to follow death.

For Christians have always looked to life after death. The eternal to-morrow has cast its shadow or light upon to-day. Epicureans might summon men to eat and drink because to-morrow they were to die, but teachers of the Christian religion have called upon men so to order their lives that death may be a door into eternal joy. When men have thought as the first Christians thought, they have not tried to forget death. Their religion has been to them the means by which death lost its sting and the grave its victory. Men, they believed, ought to live worthily of their new hopes, and express in conduct the spirit of Christ, but they were not saved by a moral régime. They were saved by a God who had sent his Son to show them the way to be saved and through their inner appropriation of His Spirit had given eternal life to those who believed upon Him.

Such a religion is no more static than life. Only as they are seen to be functional, efforts to rationalize Christian attitudes and hopes, can doctrines be understood. In every case the definitive question is not whether a doctrine is true but how successfully it coordinates religious experience with unquestioned beliefs and thus satisfies men's search for satisfaction and courage in the pursuit of the ends they seek to realize. For religion is an extension of life into help-gaining integration, like that of an organism with its environment, with those elements of the cosmic Activity with which personal relations are possible; that is with God. Christianity, let us repeat, is a technique of such integration. Its central element is he in whom such integration is held to be complete and whose experience is judged the way to freedom and deliverance from all that would hinder such union of a man with his God.

III

If the center of the Christian technique of salvation is Jesus the Christ, one outstanding element of his significance has been his death and resurrection, as means of salvation. As the crucifix and the altar focus the attention of those who enter a cathedral, so the death of Christ has been a focus of the Christian religion.

But when men have attempted to say just how this was true, and to place the death of Christ in the economy of the Christian salvation, they have followed different ways of thinking. On the one hand they have differed in the conceptions of that from which the believer was to be saved, on the other hand they have differed as to how the death of Jesus Christ helped salvation. Sometimes that from which men need to be saved has been declared to be the infinite wrath of God, sometimes the punitive justice of an infinite sovereign. Sometimes the saving significance of the death of Christ has been that of the sacrifice, sometimes that of ransom, sometimes that of the fulfillment of feudal requirements, sometimes the vicarious bearing of mankind's punishment. Viewed superficially, there seems to be no unity in these various doctrines, but viewed functionally they all serve the same end. Each had a social origin. The death of Christ has been used by the Christian thinkers to remove difficulties raised by current customs or conceptions in rationalizing the experience of salvation. The assurance-giving interpretation placed upon the death of Christ has been derived from the same pattern as that which gave rise to the question concerning the credibility or even possibility of the already experienced salvation.

The permanent values in these beliefs cast in the pattern of dominating social and religious institutions are not to be gained by new epochs of religious thought so long as they or their assumptions are accepted literally. To discover the values that lie beneath the various interpretations of the death of Christ, the historical student must study these interpretations from the point of view of social psychology. The practices and institutions embodied within them must first be discovered and their function in setting forth religious faith must be perceived. Only in this way can we see the true meaning of the death of Christ in the development of the Christian religion.

CHAPTER III

THE DEATH OF CHRIST INTERPRETED IN THE MESSIANIC PATTERN

CHRISTIANITY was not founded as an independent religion. It became such by virtue of historical circumstances. At the beginning it was the belief of a group of Jewish radicals that Jesus was the Messiah—the one whom God had empowered to be the savior of their nation and the founder of a new Jewish Empire in which the Jewish law and Jewish religion should be supreme. From the very start of the Christian religious movement Jesus was regarded as a potential savior. His full messianic work had not begun, but he was already engaged in a conflict with Satan and demons. These he was able to cast out, and this power he delegated also to a chosen group of men who were to be his particular representatives.[1] So far was he removed from any attempt at founding an independent religion that his disciples even had to ask him to teach them to pray. His followers, both during his life and later, attended the Temple and the synagogues and observed the various Mosaic rules, although they did not follow the extreme code of the Pharisees. Jesus warned them

[1] Mk. 3:23; Matt. 12:27; Mk. 1:34; Matt. 10:8; Mk. 3:15.

against these religious leaders and endeavored to inculcate the quality of religion which was represented in the Hebrew prophets.

To the members of such a movement as this the success of their founder was paramount. A savior who could not save was of course a contradiction of terms. One of the chief tasks which Jesus had to perform was that of redefining his followers' conception of the kingdom he announced and the nature of the salvation to be accomplished. At the center of this attempt at disillusionment lay the necessity of persuading men full of the revolutionary spirit to believe that the new kingdom they expected would belong to those who did not rely on violence, who loved their enemies, and who sought to treat one another with sacrificial kindness. Furthermore, he must needs prepare them for the tragedy which his methods and message involved. While they expected him to cast out demons and so break the kingdom of Satan, to set up a throne of judgment, beat down the Romans, and by supernatural power build up the kingdom of David, he was forecasting his future in quite other terms. If by the spirit of God he could cast out demons, then the kingdom of God was drawing nigh to them, but it would not come by observation or by violence. Persecution and death awaited both him and his followers. If they lost confidence in him and his messianic significance, he advised them to return home. The program which he was setting up was not for moral dilettantes. He had come to cast fire into the world, and he was impatient to see it begin to burn.[2]

I

Jesus, however, gave no teaching regarding his death.[3] He forecast it and tried to prepare his disciples' minds for the tragedy, but he did no more. Only by reading back into the gospel records the thoughts of later centuries can any teaching of an atonement by the death of Jesus be found. That Jesus regarded his death as inevitable in his work of preparing men for the coming kingdom of God is evident. That he may have felt himself the Suffering Servant may be possible.[4] But to find in his references anything in the nature of substitution or vicarious bearing of punishment is to misinterpret his sayings. Jesus saw that he could not continue his work of heralding the coming kingdom among the masses without arousing the hostility of officials and ecclesiastics. The outcome of such hostility could easily be argued from the fate of John the Baptist and the ancient prophets. He did not seek a martyr's fate, but regarded death as the will of God when once he saw it was inevitable. There must always have been present in his mind the temptation to resort to arms in the interest of the protection both of himself and his followers. At one time he even told his disciples to buy swords. But when the issue was finally

[2] Lk. 12:49.
[3] Cf. Wendt, *Teaching of Jesus*, II, 235 *seq.*
[4] Lk. 22:37.

raised and the Temple police had been led to the olive grove where he was passing the night with his disciples, he yielded himself and told Peter not to attempt armed defense.

Nor is the reason for such an attitude obscure. Jesus was preaching that God is fatherly and that those who possess the spirit of love are the true children of his kingdom. He had told his followers that they should not resist the evil man who was oppressing them, but that they should love their enemies. All of his teaching was based on his belief that love was supreme because God was love. He could not therefore consistently appeal to methods he himself condemned. He saw plainly enough that any attempt to follow his teaching, whether by himself or by others, would mean misinterpretation and persecution. And when in his own case these results appeared he endured them rather than abandon his faith that his Father would in some way give him a victory over the world. To have done otherwise would have been to recant.

Thus when Jesus refers to his death it is to be understood as an unhappy fate which, because of man's perversity, was attached to his own life of service and love. As a choice between life and this service he chose service. He gave his life as a ransom, the cost of his refusal to abandon faith in his heavenly Father. He had a baptism to be baptized with.[5] And so it was that, standing in the prospect of his immediate death, he

[5] Lk. 12:50.

could speak of it as that in which his great bequest of love was written. It was a new covenant in his blood.[6] He was ready to guarantee with his life the truth of his teaching as to the love of God. Nor is there in the synoptic gospels a trace of any other interpretation. To their writers his death was the tragic outcome of his program and his career.[7] They saw in it nothing theological or even sacrificial. It was a calamity which was the price of a supreme loyalty. That both they and Jesus regarded his life as sacrificial in the sense that he was working for others at expense to himself is beyond question. That was a dominant note in the life of Jesus. But such an expensive loyalty to love both divine and human as the supreme moral quality, seems not to have been given any further interpretation until the exigencies of a newly independent religious movement led Paul and his successors to use the death of Christ to meet difficulties which naturally arose among gentile Christians.[8]

II

Thus the point of view of the first nucleus of the Christian movement as set forth in the gospels is unlike that of their successors of a thousand years later. They shrank from thinking of their Master's death, and pre-

[6] Mk. 14:24; Matt. 26:28.
[7] Mk. 8:31; 9:30; 10:32.
[8] The attempt by Denny, *The Death of Christ,* to find traces of an expectation of a genuine atonement in various experiences of Jesus seems a theological misrepresentation of the gospel narrative.

ferred to think of his triumph. His death had to be interpreted, and that interpretation had to be within the area of their national psychology as seen in their central belief that Jesus was the future judge, the conqueror of Satan, the man from heaven, the savior of all those who believed he could save. First of all, therefore, they had to convince themselves that his death, so far from destroying, helped establish his messianic dignity.

Unfortunately we do not have material which comes directly from the church at Jerusalem. The book of Acts, however, may fairly well be trusted to have preserved the outstanding beliefs of the first Jerusalem community. Whatever may be the critical conclusions regarding the historical value of the details of the earlier chapters of Acts, it is highly improbable that any record of the first century purporting to reproduce the belief of the early apostles should have gone far wrong in the exposition of their treatment of the death of Jesus. Both Acts and Paul alike make it plain that the method by which these first Christians met the difficulty of a crucified Christ sprang from the Jewish social mind. It was the simple affirmation that the scriptures had foretold that the Christ should suffer and be raised from the dead. In the earlier forms of their teaching they do not seem to have gone beyond this discovery that the death and resurrection of Jesus fulfilled what they regarded as prophecies in the Old Testament.[9] The fact

[9] Cf. Acts. 2:25-36; 4:23-30.

that such prophecies had never been given messianic content did not weigh in their minds. They had found new knowledge of God's law and purpose in the Bible. New light had broken from the Word as they studied the scriptures from the elevation of their faith in the crucified Messiah.

The oldest literary remains of Christianity are the letters of Paul. In one to the Corinthians [10] the Apostle refers to the gospel which he said he had received and through which salvation and stability in the Christian life had come to the Christian. The first elements of this gospel he declares to be that Christ died for the sake of our sins according to the scriptures, that he was buried, that he rose on the third day according to the scriptures. This exposition of the gospel makes no reference to the teaching of Jesus, much less to any general philosophy of religion. It formulates the essential characteristic of the movement of which Paul was a leader. It of course goes without saying that Paul was a monotheist and held distinct views as to human morality, but, as he himself implies,[11] one might have these beliefs and still not enjoy the salvation which he and his fellow apostles announced. The essential guarantee of his gospel is clear—the death and the resurrection of Jesus were in fulfillment of prophecy.

In order to appreciate this position of Paul, one must bear in mind that he was a Jew writing to Gentiles who had accepted the Old Testament as the oracles of God.

[10] 1 Cor. 15:1-8.

[11] 1 Cor. 15:14, 15.

Those whom he addressed were no longer pagan, nor were they indifferent to the authority of the Jewish scriptures. So far as we can recover the early stages of the development of the Christian religion, it may be described as a transition from a sectarian movement among the Jews to a religious movement among those who, while not Jews, were yet ready to give weight to the Jewish scriptures and to certain of the Jewish hopes. The little groups of Christians which Paul founded were ethnically mixed, but if his method of thought and appeal is any criterion, they were all alike responsive to the treatment of the scriptures as possessed of an inspired authority.[12] Paul's contemporaries, Philo and Josephus, indicate clearly how the scriptures were regarded as possessed of a prophetic quality, and the early Christian apologists later were to use the scriptures frankly as oracles foretelling that which was fulfilled in the experience of Jesus.[13]

It was natural, therefore, that the Jews, who had expected the Messiah to be a triumphant conqueror, should have met the shock of disappointment caused by the death of Jesus by the use of passages of the Old Testament which seemed susceptible to such an interpretation. Both elements were in the Jewish psychology. This process had already begun, as Paul says, in the Jerusalem community. And in certain passages in the

[12] Acts 13:22-41 is an example of the apostolic method.

[13] Cf. Clement of Alexandria's repeated reference to prophecy as an oracle.

synoptic material the statements are made explicitly that it was Jesus himself, after his resurrection, who taught the disciples the necessity of the Christ's dying as foretold by the prophets.[14]

The fact that Jesus fulfilled prophecy gave no special value to his death itself. It simply established what might be called the legitimacy of death as a part of his messianic experience. Its purpose was thus more apologetic than doctrinal. The death of Jesus as the forerunner of his resurrection had been prophesied by the scriptures, and it was enough to say that his death thus strengthened his position as the Messiah.

It was, of course, inevitable that there should be further expositions of the significance of the death of Jesus, but they all sprang from the same desire to give meaning to the death of one who, by virtue of his messianic office, would be the victor rather than the victim of the controversy between God and the heavenly powers and death. The circumstance, belief, practice, or ideal that gave rise to difficulties in accepting the death of the Christ thus furnished the clew to a method of meeting the objection itself. Both alike sprang from the Jewish attitude toward the Old Testament as the prophecy of divine salvation, at first of a nation and then of those who were the prospective members of the imminent kingdom of God.

[14] Lk. 24:13-27.

CHAPTER IV

THE DEATH OF CHRIST IN THE PATTERN OF SACRIFICE

ONE pattern to express the significance of the death of Christ originated in response to a religious need felt throughout the entire world, but especially in that of Hellenism. Unlike the sublimated biology of the mystery religions, it was essentially one of ritual. Reconciliation with some god was one of the purposes of every cult. Misfortune was traced to the anger of a divine person, and reconciliation was therefore imperative if life was to be fortunate. That such a view was universal in the Roman world appears in the astonishing differentiation of polytheism and the multiplication of shrines and sacred places. Among the Jews sacrifices had been offered for centuries, but they had been centralized at Jerusalem, and Judaism as a religion was increasingly dependent upon the instruction of the synagogue rather than upon sacrifices. Such a development was the natural outcome of a religion that, believing in only one God, also believed that one city was the place in which he was particularly to be worshiped. By the time of Paul sacrifice was no longer practiced among the hundreds of thousands of Jews scattered throughout the Roman Empire. Yet the importance of the sacrifices at Jerusalem was increased, for if the multitudes of Jews could never hope to offer them to God in person, the high priest could every year sacrifice for the entire nation.

I

Christianity moved into a world which had identified the reconciliation of God and man with the offering of sacrifices. When the Christian communities began to emerge throughout the Empire, they found themselves cut off from such practices and yet dominated by the habit of sacrifice. As Christians they could not worship as Jews, much less as heathen. There was left, therefore, a social practice without corresponding Christian action. They believed that they had been reconciled with God, but no priest had ever accepted that sacrificial gift which gave dramatic expression to the establishment of reconciliation. If Christianity had been a philosophical system such a lack would not have been felt, but it was a religion in the making. At its heart was the assurance of its followers that the enmity between themselves and God due to sin with liability to the divine punishment of death had passed. They had experienced that which argued the reconciliation. Yet there had been no sacrifice.

It is not strange, therefore, that Paul, with his exceptional power of exposition, should have seen in the death of Christ something which functioned in the Christian reconciliation as the sacrifice functioned in the ritual of the altar. But the sacrificial gift (if one so believed it) was furnished not by man but by God in the interest of proclaiming the fact of his reconciliation.[1] Paul does not develop this figure, although he does at other times refer to the death of Christ in terms which are those of the sacrifice.[2] Yet it is surprising to see how seldom these references occur. Subsequent theology, under the influence of the developed doctrine of the atonement, has used his expressions to support its views, but if Paul's words be judged in the light of the first century the conception of the death of Jesus as a sacrifice is clearly that of an analogy. Strictly speaking, Jesus was not sacrificed but executed. He was offered upon no altar, by no priest, and as the gift of no man. That is to say, none of the conditions of a literal sacrifice were met. But the reality of the believer's participation in the salvation which Paul saw in Jesus' experience of death and resurrection was easily set forth in sacrificial terms.

Any understanding of Paul's thought is conditioned by the determination as to which of the various themes of his thought are really basic. That is not difficult to discover. The believer was freed from death, the penalty of sin, by virtue of possessing a life of the same

[1] Rom. 3:23-25. That the true meaning of ἱλαστήριον is not that given by most commentators (e.g., Sanday, *Romans, in loco*), but "votive gift" has been established by Deissman, *Bible Studies*, 124-35.

[2] Rom. 5:9, 10; 8:3; 2 Cor. 5:21.

kind as that which in Jesus had been shown superior to death. It is unwarranted interpretation that identifies the analogy of sacrifice with the other analogies in which the apostle sets forth the significance of Christ's death as a demonstration in history of the supreme power of the spiritual life.

It is from the point of view of Jesus' death as an element in the revelation of the way of salvation from death that we must approach the more common Pauline description of that death as being in behalf of our sins. Unfortunately the two prepositions ἀντί (in the place of) and ὑπέρ (in behalf of) have both been translated by the same word *for*. As a matter of fact, Paul in this connection never uses the former preposition which would so precisely set forth the conception of substitution. In the course of time the distinction was neglected and there sprang up the very natural but incorrect interpretation that Jesus as a sacrifice was a substitute for mankind. The proper interpretation would have been that Jesus' death was for the benefit of humanity and that this could be set forth in a variety of analogies, one of which was the conventional sacrifice. Around this vicarious work of Christ Paul's thought continually swings. The death of Jesus becomes all the more striking and significant because of its tragic form. Its purpose was part of the program of salvation which Jesus enacted. From such a point of view Paul's words become not only easily intelligible, but extraordinarily appealing. The savior had died in showing to mankind the way of salvation. His death was part of a divine plan indicative of the fact that God was already reconciled and forgiving. It was the apostle's task to set forth this fact, beseeching men in Christ's name to be reconciled to their heavenly father.[3] Substitution in any literal sense Paul did not declare. Jesus endured death, the punishment of sin, not in the place of, but in companionship with men. He who knew no sin shared in the human experience of bearing the punishment of sin as an indispensable element of his bringing men into the newness of life. The identification of this idea of participation in the common doom with the substitutionary endurance of that doom as a punishment was easy when men, under the stress of political conceptions, made the detached sayings of the apostle into theological oracles. But such an interpretation was not to come for centuries.

II

The sacrificial analogy, however, was to be literalized and made permanent in the Christian religion. Its dramatic power, the ease with which it made possible the acceptance of the Hebrew religion as the type of work of the Christ had inescapable influence in the early Christian apologetics and the later development of the Christian ritual. The writer of the letter to the Hebrews elaborates the figure. As in the Hebrew temple worship the high priest once a year offered sacrifice

[3] 2 Cor. 5:20.

for the people and entered the holy of holies, so Jesus performed the same service. Yet it was not the same but more perfect. Where the older sacrifice was that of bulls and goats, in his case it was his own body. The difficulty of his not being offered by a priest was met by saying that he himself was a priest, though not of the Aaronic line, but of the order of Melchizedek. As high priest he offered himself, an offering which was once for all and not to be repeated. Like the high priest, he went within the veil, but the temple which he entered was the life of heaven.[4]

In this interpretation we see the beginning of that acceptance of the Alexandrian method of treating the scripture which so appealed to later Christian writers. The original argument that the death of Jesus is fulfillment of scripture became identified with the apologetic desire to show that the religion of the Old Testament, which had been given by God through the prophets, was anticipatory of the experiences of Jesus. From this point of view, it was easy to speak of Jesus as bearing men's sins. But the New Testament writers do not give this conception any political or juridical quality. The analogical meaning of sacrifice would be sufficiently plain to a world that universally practiced sacrifice as a conventional element of religion. Whatever the sacrifice was understood to accomplish in the ritual of both the Hebrew and the Hellenistic worlds had been accomplished by the Christ. Jesus could be spoken of[5] as

[4] Heb. 10:1-29; 13:20.

[5] 1 Jn. 2:2.

a sacrifice, a propitiation, figuratively, just as he could be spoken of as the light of the world or the bread of life, for his death had become an element in the economy of reconciliation. That is to say, death which was interpreted as the exhibition of God's punitive wrath was now no longer to be feared by the prospective member of the kingdom of God. But this consciousness of a certain acquittal at the Judgment Day and of release from the power of sin and death depended upon the fact that, despite his innocence, Jesus himself had died in order to show in his own experience the triumphant power of that new life which the Christian himself possessed. In the sense that his death was a part of the economy of salvation from the wages of sin, he may be said to have borne out sins in his body on the tree.[6] The interpretation of his death as sacrifice is therefore to be regarded as the utilization of a pattern rather than as a literal philosophy. What the acceptance of the sacrificial gift by the priest did for the worshiper at the altar, the dying and risen Christ had done for the believer. He had given the assurance of reconciliation and pardon.

III

A most significant change, however, was to come in the Christian movement by virtue of this treatment of Jesus as a sacrifice. Apparently without any definite intention or philosophy the practice arose of treating

[6] 1 Pet. 2:24.

the common meal with which the Christians celebrated the death and the approaching return of their Master as a sacrificial meal. At the start it was a meal of communion. Christ was regarded as participating in it and Paul could warn the Corinthian Christians against participation in similar meals of the pagan gods.[7] That would be to make Christ have communion with demons. The significance of this change is not fully observable until the practice of sacrifice had disappeared from society. Then the analogy of sacrifice became a literal act, and the Eucharist developed into an actual sacrifice which the priest performs for the benefit of a congregation who feed upon the real substance of their Lord's body, broken for them. The mass is thus a continuation of sacrifice in a social order that does not practice sacrifice.

It is not easy to see how this conception of the imparted life is in any logical sense associated with Christ's death as a sacrifice, but this difficulty has had no effect on the sacrificial significance of the Eucharist. The miracle of transubstantiation wrought by the priest is followed by the presentation to God of the body and blood of Christ by the priest on an altar. It is not until that literal sacrifice has been made that the elements are taken by the priest and the worshiper. Such participation, however, does not affect the significance of the sacrifice. Whether partaken or reserved, the bread and the wine, with their substance changed to the flesh

[7] 1 Cor. 10:16-20.

and blood of Christ, are sacrificed as a means of worshiping God.

Such a practice would seem to imply that the interpretation of the death of Jesus as a sacrifice was no longer limited to his death on Calvary, and that this death was not in itself sufficient propitiation to God. Such is the claim of Protestants, and if the mass were the outgrowth of any theory it would probably be correct. A rite, however, which is the outgrowth of custom can hardly be expected to observe logical consistency. Roman Catholic theologians do not regard the sacrifice as independent of that on Calvary. "The mass can do and does no more than convey the merits of Christ to mankind by means of a sacrifice exactly as the sacraments do it without the use of sacrifice." [8] It must be admitted, however, that such rationalization seems more mystical than real. What we actually have is a rite, hallowed by centuries and given status by church action, which combines the conception of the death of Christ as a sacrifice with the idea of the memorial meal and the Hellenistic conception of the participation in the experience of God through the mystery of eating and drinking his body and blood. The task of the theologian is therefore threefold: first, to show how the elements become the real presence of Christ; second, to show how partaking of these elements brings spiritual results to the worshiper; and third, to show just how the sacrifice of Christ affects

[8] Pohle, article "Mass," in *Catholic Encyclopedia,* Vol. 10, p. 13.

God. It is the latter with which the history of Christian doctrine has been more especially concerned and around which speculation has particularly developed. But the first two problems have been none the less the subject of constant discussion. This was inevitable, for the Eucharist has always been a dramatic expression of a faith which is central in the Christian religion. It, probably more than any other element, touches the operating religion of millions of people. To take it out from the Roman Catholic or certain of the Protestant church systems would be to work a revolution, for it is the means of receiving the divine grace. The rank and file of people do not need to understand what bearing it has upon God, they only need to believe that the actual flesh and blood of Christ are present in that of which they partake. The extent to which theological argument enters into this belief will vary. In the Roman Catholic system the believer must accept transubstantiation as a dogma. With the Lutheran it is enough for him to believe the words of Christ, "This is my body, given for you for the remission of sins." The method as to how those words are fulfilled is only incidental.

This fact explains the importance of the Lord's Supper in the developing cult of the church. Any study of the significance of the death of Jesus must recognize the fact that a rite is a dramatized belief and sometimes is vastly more significant than the dogma which attempts to describe and rationalize it. A religion is more than a philosophy and includes in its technique more than intellectualism. In the development of Christianity the church has carried along its own *mores* and rites, the performance of which has been incalculably valuable as a part of the operating religion of the people at large. When a belief has become identified with a rite it is abandoned or changed with the greatest difficulty; it must be defended as necessary. In most discussions of the atonement the significance of the mass has been all but omitted, the attention of the investigator being centered on the doctrinal formulation. But it is impossible to appreciate the real position which the death of Christ has held in Christian history without laying emphasis upon the significance of the Eucharist. By it immortality was gained [9] and the rise of the importance of this rite was steady. In it, as has just been said, were preserved both the interpretation of the death of Jesus as a sacrifice and the mystery belief that it is possible to come into contact with a god by eating his flesh sacramentally. During the collapse of civilization which followed the disintegration of the western Roman Empire an uneducated people could appreciate the dramatic quality of such a rite, and its signficance was greatly enhanced by the increasing confidence in its miracle-working power. Any rationalization of this practice of the ritual performance was *ex post facto.* A custom had become so productive of religious satisfaction as to be central in an operating

[9] Irenæus, *Ag. Her.* V, 2, 2.

religion. The church had either to justify it rationally or endure a revolution. It was not merely that the Christians believed that the miracle subsequently rationalized as transsubstantiation had been wrought by the priest. They also believed that by partaking of the wafer their redemption was more assured. The divine had been physically brought into relationship with them by their partaking of the sacrament. So long as men were confident as to the efficacy of the rite, theological explanations were of only secondary importance. The practice itself was a practical interpretation. It was only when an attempt was made to solve the logical difficulties involved in the practice that doctrinal elements became permanent. Even in this regard the rite has been far more central than its rationalization.[10]

[10] The natural history of this rite is something like this. By the continued custom of the centuries it had become not only a memorial of the last supper of Jesus, but a dramatization of his statement that the bread was his flesh and the wine was his blood. The practice of the Eucharist was centered about this belief, and its value consisted largely in the actual union with the divine, made possible by the taking of the elements. As the intellectual life of Europe reasserted itself, as instruction and exhortation found their increasing place in the life of the church, it would be natural that some sort of explanation of this rite with its miraculous power should be attempted. The precise formulation of this explanation was not rapid, but it is by no means difficult to see that its constituent elements remained the same. Beneath the theology of the time lay the orthodox belief in the two natures of Christ united in one person. It was natural that this duality should be carried over to the rite which represented the presence of the real Jesus in human life.

CHAPTER V

THE DEATH OF CHRIST IN THE PATTERN OF ACQUITTAL

THE chief pattern in which the saving work of Jesus has been expressed is transcendental politics and jurisprudence. Experience in the courts gave content to beliefs concerning men's relations with God.

I

Acquittal at the coming judgment day was at the center of early Christian desire. From the point of view of strict morality, the observance of divine law, such an expectation was unwarranted. Jews as well as Gentiles had violated not only the specific statutes, but the law as law itself. They were therefore exposed to the penalties attached to such violation. The only hope which could possibly be theirs was that God might forgive the transgressor. This Paul taught was actually true in the case of those who had accepted Jesus as the Christ. This faith assured them of acquittal in the great day so soon to dawn, when God would judge the world through Christ. The guarantee of this hope was the new life due to the presence of the spirit which could cry "Abba, Father" to God.[1]

But this acquittal was something more than rhetorical or negative. It implied that its recipients were freed from the penalty to which they had been exposed. This penalty, according to Paul, was physical death, which came through sin, which in turn was the result of Adam's disobedience.[2] The expectation of the Christian could therefore be expressed in two ways; from the point of view of the messianic eschatology with its judgment day and sentences, it could be called justification or acquittal; from the point of view of actual experience and the establishment of new conditions of personal life beyond death it could be called resurrection. And this in turn involved a new quality of life before the final experience in which it should eventuate.

Pauline thought is simple. It becomes complicated only when men undertake to transform it into a philosophy and interpret detached sentences as if they were disconnected from a central hope of the conquest of death and the divine gift of a new life with a spiritual body, either through death or through change.

Yet it is precisely through this hope, which at first glance would seem to separate Paul from our modern way of thinking, that the Pauline teaching becomes most significant. For it is in this newness of life, born

[1] Gal. 4:6. [2] Rom. 5:12-21.

of the immediate contact with God's spirit that there lie new moral motives, the "fruit of the spirit."[3] This morality is not an attempt to keep statutes, but to express in conduct the motives with which it was inspired. Thus the eternal life, which reaches completion through the resurrection in a new body, had already begun. The Christian had not yet reached the full enjoyment of the newness of life, but he had already received its first installment. He had passed from death to life; he was a citizen of the heavenly places[4] with his Master, and was therefore to think the thoughts which belonged to the new life rather than to follow the impulses which sprang from his animal nature.

Such views as these can be expressed without reference to any historical events in the life of Christ. At least at the present time it is by no means uncommon to have men speak of the newness of life and the presence of the spirit of God as a means of ethical renewal without any reference to life after death, much less to the resurrection of the body. But Paul had no such way of thought. He did not reach his good news by way of philosophy. His hope was the outcome of his confidence in the reality of the experience of Jesus. If any man believed in his heart that God had raised Jesus from the dead, he was saved.[5] If Christ was not raised from the dead, the Christians' hope was vain. They were yet in their sins.[6] But if, indeed, Christ had

[3] Gal. 5:22-25.
[4] Phil. 3:20; Col. 3:1.
[5] Rom. 10:9.
[6] 1 Cor. 15:17, 18.

died and been raised from the dead, there was historical and undeniable ground for faith in one's own future. For if the spirit of the God who raised Christ Jesus from the dead dwelt in men and women, then death, the penalty of sin, had been overcome. Their bodies would be quickened by the spirit that dwelt in them. And this spirit the Christian had.[7]

If one thus looks at the center of Paul's faith, the significance of the death of Christ is clear. Paradoxical, incredible as it sounded, the Christ had died, indeed been crucified, but only thus could he ever have conquered death. Only a dead man could rise from the dead. If, therefore, the Christ were to disclose the way of salvation from death, the wages of sin, he must have been, so to speak, an exemplar. He must, like all mankind, die. He must triumph over the powers and make an exhibition of his conquest. He could be a savior only as he had demonstrated that his power which his followers shared was superior to the forces from which mankind was to be saved, and the last enemy to be overcome was death. The Christian could thank God that by his participation in death and triumph over death Jesus had shown the way by which others might share in the same victory. He was the first-fruits of those that slept.

The content of that expected acquittal at the Judgment Day is thus seen to be more than a figure of speech. Of this Paul was fully aware. Indeed, his

[7] Rom. 8:10, 11.

faith seems sometimes to have startled him. He knew that the crucified Christ was a stumbling-block to the Jew who expected a nationalist conqueror, and that it was absurd to the Greek who in his philosophical moods had long since abandoned any expectation resembling those Paul so glowingly described.[8] Yet Paul never undertakes to rationalize his hope. The gospel stood over against philosophy, foolishness to men, but since it was the foolishness of God, wiser than men. It needed no laughter of the court of the Areopagus to make the apostle realize that his message was not easy to believe. His perils and sufferings must continually have roused him to question the validity of a hope which on its face was so incredible. The answer which he would give to such queries is the quintessence of audacity. He had seen the risen Lord, a Lord who had come up from the abode of the dead and had ascended into heaven. It was not a vision, it was sight; it was not argument, it was experience; it was not philosophy, it was fact. Salvation from death had been effected and could be reproduced in those to whom the spirit of God was given when they believed as Paul believed.

When Paul gave an interpretation to the death of Jesus, it was almost as if he was founding an independent movement, so persistent and universal has been his influence upon the development of the Christian religion. His interest in Jesus as a teacher seems to have

[8] 1 Cor. 1:18-25.

been slight. He has a few "words of the Lord" but they are concerned with very practical matters like charity or divorce.[9] What interested Paul was not the historical career of Jesus but the fact that Christ, the heavenly man, had come from heaven, appeared on earth, been subjected to death, and been raised from the dead by the Spirit and thus had been set forth as indeed the son of God.[10] He did not undertake to expound a new system of philosophy or develop a socially minded body of reformers. The great fact which broke history into two parts was the revelatory inrush of the supernatural into the natural. The fact that Paul gave the same sort of ethical values to the new life of the believer that Jesus himself exemplified, that his conception of morality, like that of Jesus, was one of inwardness rather than conformity to external laws, enable us, as it were, to check his estimate as to what the mission of this supernal but humiliated being was. Jesus was no second Mithra, though, like Mithra, he was a deliverer from evil. He was no second Osiris, although his followers might expect to duplicate his master's deliverance from death. The Jesus that Paul sets forth is an historical revelation of the divine power in humanity. Jesus was the one empowered by the resident spirit of God to save his people and to found his kingdom.[11]

[9] Acts 20:35; 1 Cor. 7:10. [10] Rom. 1:4.
[11] Rom. 1:16, 24; 1 Cor. 2:5; 2 Cor. 13:4.

II

It is from this point of view that one must look at the Pauline interpretation of the death of Jesus. Justification is a formal pattern not the content of the gospels. Paul was not writing primarily to Jews. The difficulties which came from his own people's side were met by appeal to the resurrection of Jesus as the evidence that he was indeed the Messiah, but the difficulty which arose in the minds of the non-Jewish Christians was the inconsistency between this conception of Jesus and the distressing fact that he had been crucified. Paul was inevitably drawn into an attempt to adjust these two elements of his gospel. He does this in a simple fashion. Whatever significance Jesus had as the Christ he brought to his death. If one is to understand Paul it is essential that he come to the Apostle, not from the point of view of a limited human Jesus, a teacher who had fallen a victim to prejudice. There is no understanding of Paul from that point of view. Only a superhuman Christ interested him. Even if one had known Jesus after the flesh, he was to know him no longer in that capacity.[12] He heralded the one who, being in the form of God, yet not ambitious to be fully equal with God, demoted himself and became subject to death upon the cross, in order that he might save those who followed him.[13]

[12] 2 Cor. 5:16. [13] Phil. 2:5-11.

III

The death of the Christ was thus made by Paul an indispensable part of his work of salvation. By it and the resurrection he displayed the conquest of evil powers. He did not save by dying but he died because he saved. When the apostle came to set forth the significance of this fact, it steadily grew into what might be called cosmic significance. While he might hold the philosophy of his day in contempt he none the less was forced to answer questions which it propounded, and to some extent to use its terminology.

The philosophy which he faced was not that of classical Greece. One will never understand the apostle by leaping directly from Plato and Zeno to the first Christian century, or by the assumption, so easily made by certain writers, that the philosophical background of Christianity was that of the classical period of Greek thought. The philosophy with which Paul had to do was that of his own day, already on the road to Gnosticism and theosophy. It was concerned very little with the problems which Plato had confronted and very much with those of an unscientific cosmology. Eastern theosophy had penetrated Asia Minor and had built up a *melange* of thought which, while apparently never appealing to genuinely philosophical minds, was popular among the semi-literate. To such a philosophy evil was the work of supernatural powers. Human history thus became a stage on which gigantic superhuman beings ceaselessly contend. Humanity was not only the prize, but the victim, of this struggle. When, therefore, Paul undertook to appeal to the Corinthians, he very naturally put the gospel of historical fact and individual experience over against this fantastic world view. No wonder it seemed to Greeks "silly." That wisdom which the powers of this age had not known had been revealed to the followers of Christ through spiritual experience.[14] This wisdom was not, therefore, to be derived from learning or from mankind itself. It came straight from the divine Spirit to those who were living in the spirit.[15]

Yet this mysterious wisdom which the spiritual could impart to the spiritual, Paul did not undertake to set forth in detail. The death of Christ was due to the operations of these supernatural forces who thought that by putting him to death they had triumphed again and most gloriously, but death became an opportunity for the Christ to show himself the conqueror of the powers, for he rose from the dead making a spectacle of all those who had thought to overcome him.[16] After a period of struggle in which he will have broken down all the supernatural powers,[17] he will at last have overcome death itself and he will then turn over a subdued cosmos to the Father.

As Paul grew older and the pressure of the Gnostic

[14] 2 Cor. 2:6, 7; Col. 1:9; 1 Cor. 1:17-30; 2:10.
[15] 1 Cor. 2:13.
[16] Eph. 1:21; 2 Thess. 2:9; Col. 2:15.
[17] 1 Cor. 15:24.

philosophy was more distinctly felt, his thought of salvation became increasingly centered about the experience of Christ. It was not the teacher of Galilee with whom he was most concerned; it was the heavenly man, the conqueror of the heavenly powers, the victor over death, the revealer of the death-conquering Spirit. Christ becomes central in a cosmic drama in which his death was a particular definitely determined by God before creation. It was an occasion for showing the saving power of God, who raised him from the dead and set him at his right hand in heaven, above hierarchies, authorities, powers, dominions, and all other supernatural forces, who had been defeated by the Christ who had yielded to the death they inflicted only to rise and thus confound them.[18]

A mind trained in our modern ways of thought is apt to feel superior to this picture of a cosmic dualism, the elements of which are contending for mastery, the victims of which are human lives, and the conquest over which is so literal. But to one who, like Paul, does believe in them, these supernatural beings are very real and very terrible. Of course, if men came to believe that they did not exist, the terror of their power might disappear, but Paul never doubted their existence any more than he doubted the existence of demons. Humanity was at the mercy of all these powers unless

[18] Eph. 1:3-10, 19-21. For a full account of the beliefs in which as in an atmosphere the early Christians lived, see Case, *Experience with the Supernatural.*

God in some way delivered them. The Christian believed he had been delivered from them. Death to him was a prelude to a more colorful and joyous life. Therefore the heavenly powers must have been defeated and that, too, at the point where their power was most distinctly seen, namely, mortality. Without that defeat there was no hope. Philosophy did not give it; neither the Jewish nor the Greek religions gave it; but Jesus did give it. Submitting to the powers by dying, he had conquered the powers by breaking away from death. Here, then, was a gospel, a gospel of power to be shared by all those who followed Jesus, a gospel that was anything but a philosophy, a memory, or an ethic. It was the power of God unto salvation to those who believed it.[19] They shared in Christ's victory; they would duplicate his emergence from the abode of the dead; they would have the body of the resurrection.

IV

It is at this point that Paul utilized the ideas and expressions current in the Hellenistic world. While it is not clear how far the influence of Mithra worship had been felt in Syria in his day,[20] there can be no doubt that the other mystery cults had already developed there, especially those of Attis and Osiris. The Orphic cults had had their communities in Greece and Asia Minor for centuries. All of these religions gathered about the same thought, a god had died and had risen

[19] Rom. 1:16. [20] See Willoughby, *Pagan Regeneration.*

from the dead. His experience could be shared by those who had been initiated by some ritual into fellowship with himself. The experiences of the god would then be those of the initiate. Just how far such initiatory acts were regarded as having literal significance it is impossible to say, but their growing popularity in the Hellenistic period would argue that they satisfied a clearly felt want. Whatever their particular ritual may have been, these mystery religions brought to their followers the conviction that in some supernatural way they had been and would be saved from death by union with a dying and risen God.

It would be the height of historical folly to say that Paul created a belief in the resurrection from these mystery faiths. That belief, as he always insisted, came to him from his own experience, as well as from the primitive gospel. But these religions furnished him both a vocabulary and forms of thought for the exposition of the Christian's hope. As many as were baptized into Christ had put Christ on.[21] They had been buried with Christ in baptism in order that they might be raised with him.[22] As many as had been raised with Christ were to have their conduct correspond with the newness of life.[23] In one striking expression written to the Galatians he declares that he had been crucified with Christ and that the life which he lived was no longer his but Christ's.[24]

These and other similar expressions must be inter-

[21] Gal. 3:27.
[22] Rom. 6:4; Col. 2:12.
[23] Eph. 2:6; Col. 3:1.
[24] Gal. 2:20; Cf. Rom. 6:6.

patterns used by the New Testament writers, was to transform their meaning.

VI

But it would be to mutilate the New Testament thought to leave the matter at this point. So far as there is any record in the New Testament, the death of Christ was not evangelistic doctrine. Men were not asked to accept any of the interpretations given by the apostles before they could become followers of Jesus. It was enough to realize that the Christ had been crucified and buried and raised from the dead and in so doing fulfilled ancient prophecy. Such belief was followed by new religious experiences. In the eloquent words of Paul, "Old things passed away; all things became new." [27] But the change was not in the external world; it was in the life of the one who lived in that external world. He had been changed by the Spirit of God that had come into his soul. He had been freed from the penalties to which he was exposed by his violation of the law. He was to walk in freedom following the motives which would lead him to do the things which the law had tried in vain to terrify him into doing. The old nature he still carried with him in the flesh, a survival of animalism. Between these survivals and the new life there was constant struggle. It was the duty of the Christian to follow the motives of the new life and to mortify the members which were on the

[27] 2 Cor. 5:17.

earth.[28] Nor should we be indifferent to this formula. The ancient church was sensitive to that inner strife which all philosophers as observers of their kind have recognized. Man lived, as it were, on two planes, that which he shared with the animals and that which he shared with the heavenly being who had shown himself able to conquer all earthly forces and was living in the heavenly plane, a life superior to all that the world could promise. The death and resurrection of Christ therefore became the very symbol of the change of personality by which the believer passed from the motivation of the lower to the motivation of the higher life. He was to crucify his passions as Christ's body was crucified. He was to feel himself dead to the flesh and its importunities as Christ had died to the world. He was to die to the entanglement of earthly goods, but he was also, like his master, to rise into newness of life. That is to say, he was to live according to the motives furnished by his new life which were like those of Christ himself, love, joy, peace, long-suffering, gentleness, goodness, temperance.[29]

Thus the death and resurrection of Christ gave solid historical content to what might otherwise have been a poetical fancy or rhetorical form. The experience which he had undergone could also be undergone by the Christian and from this experience in the area of motivation, one became possessed of a new morality. Far enough from the legalistic phrase of their contempo-

[28] Rom. 8:13; Col. 3:5.

[29] Gal. 5:22.

raries was this self-expressing morality of Jesus and Paul, which required no law and no authority other than its own spiritual impulses. Like Jesus, Christians were living the life which was above in the heavenly order, free from any fear of punishment at the Judgment Day, superior to mortality, undismayed by their persistent struggle with those lower impulses which sought to root them to the earth.

The vanishing point, therefore, if the expression may be used, in this apostolic thought as to the death of Jesus is not worship, but conduct and character. So far is it from being true that the final outcome of religion is worship. There was, of course, worship in the Christian's life. The sense of his deliverance, the hope of his future, his sense of spiritual renewal and power to overcome the evil forces within and without him, all prompted adoration and thankfulness, but the real outcome of the Christian experience is this newness of life with its new moral qualities and ideals, the summary of which is love. It is this which gives its peculiar characteristic to the Christian religion. Not rite or law or mystery, but a life with new personal values made possible because it is at one with its God and socially dynamic because of its own motives. Such unity may be only at the expense of sacrifice of lesser goods, but it is none the less the expression of a life which is like that of God himself.

This is the experiential reality in the pattern of justification of acquittal—the abandonment of lower motives, the appropriation of spiritual power, the feeling of the consequent urge to love and sacrifice. These constitute the real content of the Christian religion according to the apostle. Their outcome was dramatized and demonstrated in the life, death and resurrection of Christ.[30]

[30] Cf. 1 Jn. chs. 1 and 2.

CHAPTER VI

THE DEATH OF CHRIST INTERPRETED IN THE PATTERN OF SONSHIP

THE development of the Christian religion subsequent to Paul followed along lines set by the creative attitudes of the Hellenistic civilization. On one side it became a world view which at least attempted to rationalize its belief in Jesus as the divine Savior, and on the other side it became a cult, the elements of which were largely supplied by popular religious practices. So far as the eastern half of the empire is concerned, the central idea of salvation became distinctly a deliverance from death and the resurrection of the body, while alongside of this was developed the importance of Jesus as the incarnation of the reason and will of God. The speculative minds of the time were far more interested in solving the relations of the historical Jesus with the Godhead than in discussing the problem of sin. The conception of the salvation from death accomplished by Jesus was given a metaphysical color by the conviction that human nature in a realistic sense had been touched by the divine and transformed. As was commonly said, by the incarnation humanity was theized and given a complete immortality. Since this incarnation was in the flesh it, too, was to share in the immortality by the resurrection of the flesh.

Such a philosophy, if the word may be used, reminds one of Paul, but is far enough from the apostle's conception. Over against his belief that believers were individually transformed by the Spirit of God into a new personal life that was moral as well as mightier than death, came the quite non-moral conception of a human nature transformed by the virgin birth and a consequent enjoyment of a resurrection in full individuality with happiness on the part of those who were believers in Christ and suffering on the part of others. From this point of view the most vital question would be the reality of the incarnation. Had the real god become man? Was it real human nature, with body and spirit, flesh and blood, in which the divine had become incarnate? The intellectual difficulties that lay in accepting this Christian hope were increased rather than diminished by various speculative efforts to avoid a divine incarnation and make the personality of Jesus an appearance. If that were true, the entire philosophy of salvation was destroyed. Unless the humanity of Jesus was real and unless God was really incarnate, the two natures (or substances) had not come in contact and humanity had not been "theized," i.e., made immortal. "Generation," the figure of sonship became central in theological thought.

I

Thus interpreted, the conception of salvation led the church to emphasize the actuality of the body of Jesus as well as all the other elements of his human personality. The first Epistle of John makes it a test of a believer's salvation;[1] Barnabas declares that the Lord endured to deliver his flesh to destruction that by the remission of our sins we might be sanctified by the blood of his sprinkling.[2]

Clement declares on account "of the love which he had for us Jesus Christ, our Lord, gave his blood on our behalf and his flesh for our flesh and his life for our life."[3]

Such a statement is only an extreme formula for an element in the early conception of salvation. This, it will be recalled, was not forensic, but one might say biological. However much the early church writers conceived of man's relations to God under the general patterns of government, and however ready they may have been to use the Jewish conceptions of the Day of Judgment and of the justification, that is to say, the acquittal of the believer, the content of the salvation which they expected centered about the rendering of human nature, including the flesh as well as the spirit of man, superior to death. From this point of view the death of Christ got its chief significance in the Apos-

[1] 1 Jn. 4:2, 3. [2] Barnabas, *Ep.* v, 1, 6.
[3] 1 Clement, xlix, 6.

tolic Fathers as well as in Paul. With them, as with the apostle, resurrection from the dead was needed if prophecies were to be fulfilled.[4]

As one might expect, these early Christian writers make use of the death of Christ as an incentive to Christians. In it he showed that humility that Christians should have,[5] and gave an illustration of the self-sacrifice which his followers also should exhibit. But these considerations are not central in the valuation of the death of Jesus; like the child-bearing of the virgin Mary it remained one of the mysteries of the religion.[6] Yet even as a mystery it is an integral part of the complete work of Jesus which was centered around the incarnation, with the consequent transformation of human nature through contact with the divine. The regeneration of the individual consequent to his acceptance of this work of Jesus was symbolized by or possibly due to the baptism which was the laver of immortality and the participation in the Lord's Supper, where one ate the bread of immortality. In these early writers the interpretative pattern of sacrifice is frequently met, but it does not become central and the Eucharist has not be-

[4] As clear a statement of this as any is to be found in the *Epistle of Barnabas* V, 6, 7. Christ endured in order to destroy death and to show forth the resurrection from the dead, because it was necessary for him to be manifested in the flesh, in order that he might both fulfill the promise to the fathers and might show, while he was upon the earth, that as he had accomplished the resurrection, so he would himself conduct the judgment.

[5] 1 Clement, xvi, 17.

[6] Ignatius, *Eph.* xix, 1.

come more than a memorial meal.[7] In all this the central teaching of Paul can be seen.[8] The death and the resurrection of Jesus are illustrations of the actual experience which the believer is to have. But no clear statements are made as to the bearing of the death of Christ upon God's action in making such salvation possible. Apparently it was enough for them to feel that the work of Jesus was due to the love of the Father.

From such a view of salvation it was inevitable that Christian thought should extend to those who were dead at the appearance of the Christ. What was to be expected in their case? Could those who had died before the gospel had been preached also share in the resurrection from the dead?

This difficulty was already in the minds of the Christians of Paul's time,[9] but apparently his words concerned only the Christians who had died. The question of others who in the past had died was not necessary. Concern as regards them appears in 1 Peter,[10] where there is the first reference to any work of Jesus among the dead. There he is said to have preached even to

[7] See Justin Martyr, *Apology*.

[8] Rashdall, *Idea of Atonement in Christian Theology*, p. 195, properly notes that in the apostolic fathers there is little trace of "St. Paul's distinctive doctrine of justification by death apart from works." As a statement of omissions in the apostolic fathers the statement is correct, but any interpreter of Paul will be likely to be led astray if he makes the justification of faith the central thought in the Pauline conception of salvation. That, as has been pointed out, is the transformation of the believer by the Holy Spirit.

[9] 1 Thess. 4:13-5:11.

[10] 3:18-20.

the dead who lived before the flood. This projection of the saving power of the incarnation into the abode of the dead is thoroughly logical, as repeatedly appears in the different writers. In none does this more clearly appear than in the discussion of Irenæus. To this interesting father the death of Jesus was the continuation of his historical activity. As his one great purpose was the giving of immortality to humanity through the union of the human and divine in the incarnation,[11] so his visit to the underworld was for the purpose of completing the salvation by delivering the dead from the control of the Apostasy, as Irenæus calls Satan. But in their case the situation was somewhat different from that of living persons. The claims of the Apostasy to the control of the dead had to be met. These claims were rooted in the disobedience of Adam, which apparently passed over, in Irenæus's opinion, to humanity itself. Jesus, in whom the divine transformed humanity, recapitulated the history of humanity at each of its stages, facing conditions which humanity had successively faced, but always being obedient where humanity had been disobedient. In a striking passage[12] he describes how Jesus, in order to save all through himself, passed through every age, an infant for infants, a child for children, a young man for young men,

[11] Irenæus, *Ag. Her.* III, 18, 7; 19, 1.

[12] *Ag. Her.* ii, 22, 4. See also iii, 22, 4; v, 16, 3; 17, 1-4. This recapitulation was a favorite thought with many of the Fathers.

and old man for old men. His death thus would be a continuation of the series, and as by his action he saved persons of the other groups, dying he saved those who were dead. In freeing the dead from the control of Satan, Jesus died in order to complete the recapitulation and so to reach the underworld and persuade the Apostasy to release the dead. Thus it was that he "redeemed us from it by his blood." [13] But it is to be noted that this redemption has nothing to do with God, but is from Satan.

This identification of Satan with Pluto, the Hellenistic god of the underworld, is a phase of the far-reaching process by which the attributes of the gods of paganism were appropriated by Christianity.[14] In the days of Irenæus, the dread figure of the Apostasy had not become the devil of the Middle Ages, although he was regarded as the rebel from heaven. Just how he got possession of the abode of the departed spirits it is not possible to say, but that such was the case seems to have been universally believed by the Christians. Satan would thus have within his control all humanity, either prospectively, or, as in the case of the Old Testament worthies, actually. The rescue of those thus subject to its lord furnished the motive for the visit of Jesus to the underworld through dying.

[13] *Ag. Her.* v, 2, 1; iv, 42, 3.

[14] Perhaps the most striking illustration of that is the transference of the attributes of Cybele and other female divinities to Mary, the mother of Jesus.

II

This projection of the saving power of the incarnation into the abode of the dead is a logical elaboration of the recapitulation theory as to the work of Christ, but it never became a central doctrine of the church. In its place was a more highly dramatized account of the visit of Jesus to the underworld which gained wide publicity in western Christendom. Mankind was regarded as being under obligation to the devil because of sin, and this debt God himself had to recognize. The death of Christ was the paying of the debt to Satan.[15] But the Fathers leave obscure just how the death of Christ could be a payment or satisfaction of the debt which humanity owed. Irenæus speaks of the Christ's appeal to "persuasion" as befitted his character and purpose.[16] But he also regards the work of Christ as that of deifying human nature by the incarnation and so enabling it to overcome Satan.[17] This latter view is more central in Irenæus than the persuasion of Satan. He does not speak of Jesus as being made a ransom to Satan.[18] Pauline thought is thus more in evidence in Irenæus than has sometimes been claimed, although he regards humanity more realistically than did the apostle. In Christ humanity repudiates Satan and is freed from his control.

[15] See passages from Ambrose in Frank, *History of the Doctrine and Work of Christ,* 109 *seq.*

[16] *Ag. Her.* v, 1, 1.

[17] *Ag. Her.* iii, 18, 7; 19, 1.

[18] Cf. the quotations given by Rashdall, *op. cit.,* 216, 217.

In this teaching of Irenæus there is a noticeable high morality in the relations of Christ and Satan. But it was not to continue. As the Western world was submerged under the rising brutality of the repopulation of the Western Empire by German tribes, the deliverance was said to have been accomplished by the deceitful methods of the time. God is represented as having made a bargain with Satan by which Jesus is to be substituted for the dead saints in Satan's power. To this Satan agrees without knowing that Jesus was the incarnation of God. The exchange is made and Satan permits the dead to escape.[19] The unethical quality of the act of God in deceiving Satan was frankly admitted by Pope Gregory and Epiphanius, who did not apparently feel any moral difficulty in the case. In this the conscience of the Latins seems not to have been so sensitive as in the case of the Greeks, for Gregory of Nyssa, who adopts the theory, justifies it by claiming that Satan was himself a deceiver and would be shown the wickedness of deception by his experience—for Gregory of Nyssa hoped that the devil would be ultimately saved. On the other hand, Gregory of Nazianzin protested against the entire transaction by which any ransom should be paid the devil.[20] The other great Cappadocian, Basil, and Chrysostom, did not

[19] This idea of the deception of the devil by God is certainly as old as Gregory of Nyssa, who is apparently the originator of the famous analogy by which the devil is said, in grasping at the bait of Christ's humanity, to have been caught on the hook of his deity.

[20] *Oration* xlv, 22.

seem to feel the same scruples, the latter working out in considerable detail the justice of the payment of a debt to Satan by the death of Christ. The full details of the visit of Christ to the underworld were worked out in the fifth century in the *Gospel of Nicodemus.*

Yet it probably would be a mistake to think of this dramatization of the dealings of God with Satan as at first more than what the Jewish rabbis would call *haggada,* that is, a homiletic story intended to carry some truth. Throughout the entire patristic period this visualized theology is paralleled by the more philosophical conceptions of the necessity of Jesus passing triumphantly through all the experiences in which humanity had failed and of the religious conception of Jesus' death as a sacrifice. It was only a morally disintegrated social order that could make its practices of ransom into a theological pattern.

CHAPTER VII

THE RISE OF THE IMPERIAL PATTERN IN WESTERN CHRISTIANITY

THE corollaries of the doctrine dealing with the incarnation were never equal to the task of controlling the development of Christian theology. They have remained, however, a very important element in the cult of Christians. Baptism has been the laver of immortality, the Lord's Supper the bread of immortality, and the resurrection of the flesh from the grave is promised in every burial service of historic churches. But this attainment of resurrection of the entire man, body as well as spirit, is more akin to scientific than to ethical interest. The belief that the unsaved would be punished in the next world in the agonies of being burned forever was universal in the Christian communities of the Middle Ages, but it was not systematically correlated with morals. The necessity of an incarnation for the purpose of transforming mortal human nature was that around which the Christian thought seems to have centered. Nor is it difficult to understand why this was the case. Ecumenical theology preserves the answers given the intellectual problems raised in the

Hellenistic world. The metaphysical questions which brought about the Council of Nicea were the outcome of a disputatious rather than a constructive social mind. Only in a society indifferent to politics, but with plenty of leisure for theological discussion, could disagreement as to the metaphysics of the Son, the Father, and the Holy Spirit have threatened the peace of an empire. The great interests and discussions of the patristic period are centered on issues wholly outside of social experience, such as whether the Son, the Father, and the Holy Spirit are of the same substance, the relation of the three personæ of the Trinity, the number of natures, persons, and wills possessed by the historic Jesus, whether the Holy Ghost proceeds from the Father or from the Ftaher and the Son. These are the questions which divided the church for centuries, and it is the answers to such questions that constitute all of the ecumenical creeds. There is no one of them that enters the realm of morals or endeavors in any way to expound the relations of man to God—and that, too, in the face of the fact that a Christian morality was evolving.

I

The explanation of this lies in the social psychology of the Eastern Empire. It had no genius for politics, and long before the foundation of Christianity it had submitted itself to the government of Rome. Whatever local government it may have had was almost entirely concerned with non-political affairs like the organization of the worship of some deity.[1] It was inevitable therefore, that the intellectual interest should deal chiefly with non-political matters permitted by the Roman administration and that politics should not have been creative in the general thought of the Eastern Empire. And therefore it is understandable how the pattern of the Eastern theology should have centered around the idea of natures and, generation rather than around guilt and law. This would be true notwithstanding that the political pattern really was an element in theological thought. All biblical thought is expressed in governmental analogies and metaphors. Even when Jahweh is spoken of as the Father, it is as the founder and the head of the nation. More than that, the governmental relationships of God were constantly in the minds of the philosophers and of Christians. They reappear in the highly educated teachers of the church. Origen, for instance, speaks of the laws of nature of which God is the legislator.[2] The references to God as king and lawgiver are very common, but this pattern does not seem to have been theologically productive. The interests of the Christians in the East were not political.

II

In the western half of the Roman Empire, however,

[1] For a full discussion of the political situation in the East and in Asia Minor in particular, reference may be made to Mitteis, *Reichsrecht und Volksrecht*, and Ramsay, *The Church in the Roman Empire*, chs. ix, x.

[2] *Against Celsus*, V, 33.

the situation was radically different. In the East Roman imperialism was administrative; in the West it was creative. In the East Rome superimposed its control over nations older than itself; in the West it built up a civilization in much the same way that England built up a civilization on the American continent. How thoroughly ingrained was the political mind-set of the West will appear from the contrast between the power of the two halves of the Empire to recover from destruction. Both halves of the Empire suffered a similar, though not contemporaneous fate in being submerged by foreign peoples. In the West, however, the Roman ideas had such vitality as to survive the confusion of the barbarian invasion and to reorganize a civilization. In the East, after the barbarian and Turkish invasions, little was left of Roman institutions. Probably the chief cause for the continuance of Roman influence in the West was the Catholic Church. In it was preserved the very genius of the Empire. The organization of the dioceses, the legal structure of the church, indeed, the entire conception of the church as an imperial unity are indications of the control which the imperial system had over the minds of men and over the church in particular. It was inevitable that such a basic political experience should become a theological pattern. The Western literature is controlled by a theological conception which is a transcendentalized imperialism. And this theology was the obverse of its institutional history. From the days of Cyprian to those of Innocent III Rome was developing an ecclesiastical empire. Imperialism was the one pattern in which should be set forth not only relations of Christians but also of God and his world.

It was Augustine who really lifted the Roman state into theology. Into a political conception born of the simple state of the Hebrews he poured a content that was derived from the majestic figure who ruled the world from Constantinople and Rome. To him God was no longer Jahweh of Zion, but the absolute ruler of the universe. Lacking anything like to-day's knowledge of the physical universe, he was naturally controlled by that political miracle of human history under whose protection he lived. The fact that by his day this earthly sovereign was losing his power to enforce his laws and protect his subjects seems to have stimulated Augustine to think of God as a ruler whose power was unlimited and whose will could not be nullified by the action of any creature. While it is true that in some of his most significant writings he uses comparisons based on psychology, the right of God to determine whatever he wished was basic in his thought. It leaps repeatedly into expression in the *Confessions* and is far more constructive in his thought than his rather perfunctory discussion of the Trinity. Augustine believed in the Trinity, for so the church had decided. He discussed the Trinity at length, but when he thought about religion as distinct from dogma, his mind invariably used the categories of politics.

The outstanding illustration of this attitude is, of course, his treatise on the *City of God*. The entire work is, in fact, a defense of the belief that the God whom the Christians worship is the real governor of the world, able to protect his people. Such a faith had been sorely shaken by the capture of Rome by the Goths, and there were those who said that this miracle of misfortune was due to the fact that Rome had abandoned its ancient gods and had turned to the Christian God. Augustine's treatise is an answer to this charge, and in it he develops a philosophy of history which is an extension of political thought. God's kingdom had been growing always in the world, though opposed by the powers of evil. God carried it forward through the Hebrew people and will complete it in the triumph of Christ. Through it all his relations to the world are set forth as akin to those of the emperor to the empire.

Two relations particularly developed by Augustine are supplementary to each other. On the one side he speaks of the absolute law of God and on the other side of the utter hopelessness and guilt of humanity originally created by God to be his loyal subjects. The first of these two interests accounts for Augustine's interest in the freedom of the will and the responsibility of men. His language is sometimes such as to lead to the inference that man had no freedom of the will; on the other hand, when he discusses the matter frankly he protects the freedom of the will at the expense of human nature itself.

It is at this point that the real significance of the Western influence of political adventure and development appear, for the dominance of the political pattern in Augustine's discussion of the relation of man and God quite overshadows the older interest in salvation as the giving of immortality to the body and soul of man. In this belief Augustine certainly shared, and he discussed it to some extent, but he accepted it as he accepted the Nicene creed, something a churchman could be expected to believe. His interest, as he himself said, was in the relation of God and man. This he included in his political pattern, and his influence made Western Christianity different from the Eastern. From his day to this the starting point of Western orthodoxy has been sin—a violation of a command of God by Adam which brought not only corruption but guilt upon an entire race. The interest of the speculative East in substance and the Trinity reappears in the Western theology, but the real problem of the church life of the West from the days of Augustine has consisted in developing a technique by which men could be delivered from the punishment which they deserved as members of a guilty race.

III

It would not be correct to say that Augustine was the first to emphasize evil in human nature, but he is responsible for the pessimism which is the starting point of all later theology. Nor is it difficult to understand how this should be the case. He lived in the very midst of a collapsing civilization. Western Europe was being overrun by new races. Cities were being looted, libraries destroyed, works of art ruined, men and women killed or enslaved. The accumulated culture of centuries was being all but annihilated. Is it any wonder that Augustine should have been hopeless regarding human nature? But the influence of social débacle is not so much in Augustine's thought as his own reading of human motives. He never escaped the influence of his Manichean experience, and as he grew older he tended to see evil in desire, especially in sex. Without any knowledge of biological law he believed that Adam transmitted to his descendants his moral characteristic acquired by the disobedience of the command of God. Every human soul ever born had been born damned to the fires of hell, and, because the corruption of its nature had rendered it incapable, without God's help, of choosing the right, the punishment threatened Adam was passed on to his descendants. This is the base line of all Western orthodoxy from Augustine's day to this. He used the words of Paul, but he made Pauline rhetoric into a theological system. Men were saved, but the reason for their good fortune lay in the mystery of God's grace. No man unaided was capable of acquiring the innocence which belonged to the image of God which Adam had lost by his disobedience.

On this hopelessness and helplessness of mankind

Western orthodoxy has built itself. The moral impotence of man makes the church indispensable as the purveyor of God's grace. To Augustine and his successors the work of the church was something much more concrete than the heralding of truth. Truth it possessed, but it had something more, namely, the miracle-working power of the saints and of Christ and his mother. Yet Augustine and the Christians of the centuries that immediately followed him did not locate the death of Christ in any relationship to this massive theological structure. The consubstantiability of the Son and the Father in the Trinity, had become dogma and the person of the historical Jesus was in the West already moving toward the decisions of Chalcedon. The death of Jesus one might almost say was incidental in the thought of Augustine. He makes little use of it except in the way of picturing Jesus as a ransom to Satan. His resurrection furnishes certain material of illustration for hope of the flesh, but Augustine does not treat the death of Christ as among the main theological entities. He is more interested in psychology than in theology. Not until Europe began once more to construct a civilization did the death of Jesus gain doctrinal significance in Christian theology. He had died as a sacrifice for the living and as a ransom to Satan for the dead. He was interceding with the Father for his people, but there was not sufficient creative interest in the collapsing Roman world to demand any vindication of the pardon which Augustine had so extolled. Government, indeed, was for centuries to be a problem rather than a creative influence. During those dark years the church carried on its work with little concern as to the right of God to forgive members of a guilty and condemned race. It had the apparatus of salvation at its disposal, and by sacrament, creed, and almsgiving it mediated the grace of God to a world untroubled by speculative questions as to the honor or punitive justice of the God it feared.

CHAPTER VIII

THE DEATH OF CHRIST IN THE PATTERN OF FEUDALISM

THE Christian religion is more than Christian theology. As a technique of salvation it is primarily concerned with the methods and agencies by which human life becomes at one with God and so is transformed. From the point of view of philosophy this relationship with God is actual, even though a man be not technically religious. It would be quite impossible to think of God as actually existing and utterly indifferent to the universe. One might as well think of the air as having no relationship with plants and animals. But just as there is an intelligent way of using air and sunlight in agriculture, so is there an intelligent way of co-operation between man and God. In a period of illiteracy this will be reduced by the learned to actions and rites and such a minimum of creedal statement as is essential for the maintenance of religious uniformity. To the thousands of ignorant, brutalized northern immigrants who had settled in the western half of the Roman Empire the discussion of the synods and councils must have been all but unintelligible. What understanding could those fierce Franks who march across the pages of Gregory of Tours have with the discussion as to adoptionism, or the serfs who tilled the fields of the newly rising nobility of Charlemagne's time with those discussions over free will which cost the monk John Gottschalk his liberty?

However the learned or semi-learned might discuss various items of the developing theological system, religious practices multiplied. Ignorance always breeds superstition and multiplies superhuman beings. The fears of the Middle Ages were enlarged by homiletical ingenuity until the world was again filled with supernatural beings that needed to be defeated or placated. Devils waited in every dark corner and evil spirits found their victims in the forests. The world, all but without means of illuminating darkness, found its terror multiplied by all those happenings that darkness covers. In the church there was to be found deliverance from dangers, though unfortunately without the removal of the objects of fear. Baptism soon after birth, prayers to some saint whose favor had been urged by a dedicatory gift, confessions to the priest with consequent absolution, attendance upon church with its highly dramatic services, the retiring from the world into monastery or convent, the giving of alms, the performance of penance, all these went to make up the operating religious life of the Christian. But they were all secondary to those practices by which the believer was in a real sense brought into contact with the dead and risen Lord. The sacrifice of Calvary was repeated at the altar of every church. The priest was able by the superhuman power given him by ordination to change the substance of the bread and wine into the substance of the body and blood of Christ. These the believer took into his mouth, thus appropriating divinity. This miracle was the center of the Christian religion. The recipient must have prepared for this sacred experience, but nothing which he could do or the priest enforce had such significance as this literal union of the believer with Christ. In the flesh of Christ the deity was still incarnate and the believer shared in its influence.

For nearly a thousand years these practices continued without any attempt to answer the question as to why they had come into existence. The church carried forward and expanded its own practices and gave to them supernatural value. Its intellectual interest was circumscribed by the biblical material, and efforts to persuade the non-Christian in the spirit of the apologists of the second century had been replaced by the zeal of the missionary, who carried the message of salvation and the means of grace to peoples even wilder than those from whom he came forth. Yet, as medieval society began to struggle out from the incredible brutalities and disorders of the Dark Ages, it found itself confronted not only with the internecine struggle with heresy, but also with a relatively highly developed culture mediated by the Arabian and the Jew. It is difficult for us to realize that for centuries science and other elements of culture came from the Arabic civilization; the philosophy of Aristotle, the art of medicine, the philosophy of the East and of Greece, education, beginnings of banking and commerce, and the amenities of civilization mostly reached the western European peoples of the Middle Ages by the way of Jews and Arabs of Spain. Long before universities had begun to appear in Europe the Christian thinker found himself confronted by opponents who were more than his equal in intelligence and training and yet who did not share in his loyalty to the New Testament and the rites and doctrines of the church. They were not Christians, but zealous supporters of two rival religions. It was natural, therefore, that there should arise the need of an argument that should be able to substantiate the central position of Christianity relative to the incarnation by some line of argument that did not rest upon a common acceptance of biblical or ecclesiastical authority. Unless it could be shown that the incarnation, so indispensable for the rite of the mass, was reasonable on its own basis rather than that of loyalty to a religion, the Christian apologist would always be at a disadvantage. It was natural, therefore, that there should be organized an argument which would appeal to the so-called infidel Moslem and Jew without first compelling them to accept the New Testament as final authority. The outstanding figure in this attempt to base Christianity itself, both on its operative and its creedal aspects, upon *a priori*, non-Christian grounds was

Anselm. As the first of the schoolmen, he represents that position which was to be so influential, namely, that while the truths of Christianity would not be known except by revelation, when once known they are susceptible of rational defense.

I

The methods of thought which Anselm adopts in his attempt to show the reason for the incarnation without any appeal to Christian sources can hardly be appreciated until one locates him in the course of medieval history, and perceives how closely he was allied with the creative social mind of his time. First of all, it is necessary to realize that the Middle Ages was a time of reorganization of a civilization. The old Roman world which had developed so remarkably in western Europe had broken down under the armed immigration of northern tribes. Cities had been destroyed; the older population had been largely killed or reduced to serfdom; the art of writing had almost disappeared. The new peoples who appropriated the remains of the civilization they had destroyed were utterly without any of the political institutions or ideas which had characterized the great age of Roman imperialism. Society reverted to an almost savage state. Commerce disappeared, officials were killed, laws were neither understood nor observed, and the only elements which seemed capable of giving any semblance of social order were represented by the military control of land.

The stronger soldier seized land on which he let weaker soldiers live in return for stipulated service. There were no taxes, there were no courts, one had almost said there was no government. What emerged out of the disorder of the seventh and eight centuries was a large number of feudal centers in which the relationship between the higher and the lower lord was a curious combination of the functions of the landlord, the military commander, and the guardian. How far any control could be exercised would be determined in the long run by the ability of the lord to maintain his status as superior to the vassal. Whatever system there was in feudalism centered around the recognition of the relative honor or dignity of the parties who entered into the feudal relationship.

In a world where old political forms had disappeared and governmental sanctions were no longer effective, this rough and ready nucleating of society was the one hope of order. Charlemagne was able during his lifetime to maintain a sort of ghostlike resurrection of the imperial system, but none of his successors could carry it on. While the names might continue and emperors might be crowned, the one tendency which was actually evolving social order was the principle of feudalism. It was not a system in the sense that it was deduced from a political philosophy, but it was a way of establishing foci of order by the establishment of a hierarchy of masters. In theory there would be at one end the king and at the other end the serf who was practically without rights, but whose labors supported the entire social structure. To recognize the relationship of protection on the one side and loyal obedience on the other was indispensable. Once weaken the dignity of the superior, and whatever social unity emerged or depended upon the obedience of the inferior was threatened. Anything like democracy would have meant anarchy.

It is easy to see, therefore, why to the men of the Middle Ages the maintenance of these different gradations of dignity and control was unquestioned. It was one of those ultimate elements of life which were the foundation upon which all political thought could be built. It did not need to be argued because it did not occur to anyone to question it. When these questions did arise in the eighteenth century, and the basic structure of a feudal society was challenged, the new era of democracy had dawned. But to have declared that all men were created equal would have seemed to the Middle Ages to be as absurd and dangerous as to say at the present time that slavery is essential to an economic order. The very preservation of society depended upon the subjection of the smaller to the greater. Obedience was the indispensable correlate of protection.

Anselm was a child of this social order and had an experience which tested its power. No sooner had he been appointed archbishop of Canterbury (1093) than he found himself in conflict with William Rufus, who was exploiting the feudal elements in the English church for his own advantage. The struggles which followed the refusal of the king to recognize Urban II as Pope found Anselm able to rely on the barons as opposed to the bishops. Indeed, it would be true to say that throughout a large part of his life he was involved in struggles upon which feudal customs like that of investiture were unquestionably the beginnings of argument.

It was this creative and controlling premise of political practice which Anselm employed in his argument to show why God became a man. From the point of view of a feudal society the argument is intelligible and convincing. Humanity had disobeyed God and in so doing had rendered an affront to his dignity. Until this affront had been satisfied by some act on the part of humanity in excess of the obedience which was also to be rendered, God was under the necessity of punishing mankind. However God might desire to select men to complete the number of the angels, depleted by the fall of Satan and followers, or however much he might love his creatures, he could not forgive until satisfaction had been rendered to his dignity. Until then he must needs punish. But he did not wish to punish all mankind, and so was ready to accept such satisfaction as might be available.

The feudal pattern of Anselm's thought reaches its inevitable *impasse*. Satisfaction can be rendered by none other than humanity, but humanity is incapable of rendering such satisfaction, not only since it continues sinful, but because the dignity of God is infinite. Yet just at this point appears the reason for the incarnation. The second person of the Trinity, very God of very God, becomes incarnate and as the God-man suffers and dies to render God's honor the satisfaction required of humanity. As man he was able to meet the requirement that mankind should render the satisfaction, and as God he was able to give his sufferings a value sufficient to make satisfaction effective.

Here, then, would be a reason for the incarnation: the impossibility of God's forgiving human sin had he himself not become incarnate. And he had forgiven believers.

Contemporary feudalism of Anselm's time completes his theory as to the way in which the sinner can gain the forgiveness which the suffering of the God-man makes God free to give. Here again the social practice becomes the unquestioned pattern of thought. Since the God-man had not sinned there was no disobedience of his own for which he had to render satisfaction, nor was he under any compulsion to suffer and die. Since he had done this for the advantage of God, he had a right to claim a boon from the Father whose desires he had thus furthered. This boon was that those who were to take the place of the angels and enjoy the blessings of heavenly salvation should be those who were his own followers.

How perfectly all this conforms to the general practices of feudalism is sufficiently apparent. That these practices may have in some way embodied the surviving elements of the old Roman law is entirely possible, but the whole motif of the drama of salvation as Anselm describes it is to be found in the dominant practice of his own time. The difficulties in which God finds himself when he wants to forget his obligation to punish until his dignity has been satisfied, the possibility on the part of the God-man's doing that for God which he did not need to do and so having the right to ask a boon, are all elements of a feudal social order. The fact that there are similarities also between the thought of Anselm and the penitential system which was then beginning to shape itself do not affect the chief consideration, namely, understanding the action of God by recourse to unquestioned basic social practices and theories. God's difficulty in forgiveness, itself born of feudal practices, is met by the utilization of the elements in the social order by which similar difficulties were met. The Anselmic interpretation of the death of Jesus is sublimated feudalism. In presenting it he never quotes Scripture, nor is there anything in the New Testament that would suggest the inability of God to forgive until his honor had been satisfied.

The new value thus given the death of Jesus by Anselm was to persist in the Christian thought and finally in modified form to develop into Protestant orthodoxy. Since the days of Anselm the death of the Christ has been regarded as having a bearing upon God and as a condition of the forgiveness which He might exercise.[1]

In Anselm's own day the theory was not altogether popular. It certainly never was made into dogma, nor was it accepted as official theology. Its basic conception, however, was to continue, and the necessity of the death of Jesus as a means of justifying God's act of forgiveness became an assumption of theological thought. To the Schoolmen there was only one serious question. Was the death of Jesus the only possible way of satisfying the divine dignity or was it one among many possible ways which God chose to accept as satisfactory? The Realists reached the former and the Nominalists the latter view. But both agreed that the death of Christ did render a satisfaction to the dignity of God which would otherwise have been unsatisfied, leaving him under the compulsion to punish a disobedient humanity.

II

It would hardly be expected that the thought of nearly a thousand years should be without its variations, and so long as the significance of the death of Christ had not been given the dignity of a dogma the

[1] For a sketch of the influence of Anselm's doctrine upon later doctrines of the atonement, see Foley, *St. Anselm's Doctrine of the Atonement.*

variety of explanation was inevitable. Yet during the Middle Ages any variation of opinion as to the meaning of the death of Christ was within the limits set by the practice of the mass. The motive of the death of Jesus had to be found in some element which contributed to the Christian salvation. The most original exposition is, as one might expect, that of Abelard who was altogether too keen a thinker either to regard Jesus as a ransom to the devil or even to accept the feudal theory of Anselm. To him the purpose of the incarnation was that God "might illuminate the world by his wisdom and excite it to love of himself." "Our redemption is that supreme love of Christ shown to us by his passion which not only frees us from slavery to sin, but acquires for us the true liberty of the sons of God."[2] This of course is very similar to what later was commonly called the moral influence theory of the atonement, and it was condemned by the Council of Saens in 1141. But as in the case of other positions taken by Abelard, it seems to have been held by that adventurous thinker as an explanation rather than as a substitute for the more common view of ransom to the devil. It was not without its influence, for already at least similar views were held by an occasional Schoolman like the English Robert Pullen. But such a view could hardly hope to compete successfully with the developing extension of

[2] Quoted by Rashdall, *The Idea of Atonement in Christian Theology*, p. 358.

the penitential system to the church. The more the church insisted on penance as a condition of justification, the more did the idea of merit for supererogatory works on the part of men and Christ become an intelligible pattern for thinking of the death of Christ. Such a tendency had the practical advantage of being administered by the church as an ecclesiastical prerogative.

III

Only as the growing intellectual life of scholasticism came to reject the idea of ransom to the devil as immoral did belief gain credence that by his death the sinless Jesus had acquired a merit which could be transferred by the church to the repentant believer. These merits at the disposition of the church were limitless and formed a distinct asset for the expansion of the doctrine of salvation. Within it there was nothing inconsistent in the doctrine of the mass or the Anselmic theory of satisfaction rendered to the dignity of God. On the contrary, it supplemented both and brought the work of Christ into even more intimate association with Christian technique. Indeed, so intelligible became this conception of transferable merits of Christ that it was to hold sway for centuries and even in Protestant theology. The simplest mind could grasp it, for it utilized the dominant practice as a pattern. If to do something extra in the way of penance had value for the penitent who had sinned, the more merit would attend the complete suffering of one who did not need the penance for himself. That advantage could be transferred for the advantage of others.

It is hardly necessary to call attention to the fundamental error in such a view of morality. Duty must always be as great as one's ability and responsibility. No one, not even Christ himself, could be better than he needed to be. The conception of merit, to say nothing of transferable quantum of merit, is denied by this very simple fact. If Jesus could be a savior, he could do nothing less than save. Morally speaking, there was no choice in the matter. That he endured suffering and death may have been an act of heroism, but to have chosen his own comfort in preference to his vocation would have been sin.

But in the use of the death of Christ by the church the homiletic value of the idea of merit because of Christ's suffering was too great to be ignored. In the liturgy which, with the sacraments and the repetition of the creeds, formed the religious activity of the masses, constant use is made of the sufferings and death of Jesus as the basis of an appeal to God for mercy. The illiterate people could be expected to cry, "Good Lord, deliver us," as the priest recited the facts of the death of Christ and prayed "By thine agony and bloody sweat, by thy cross and passion, by thy precious death and burial." In certain of the litanies the sufferings were still further specified. In fact, the purpose of the liturgy was in so small part a combination of theological belief with the prayer for mercy.

Such a practical use of the death of Jesus as furnishing an appeal to God's mercy and merits which could be applied to otherwise hopeless sinners did not prevent discussion on the part of the theologians. As we have already seen, there was still the question as to whether the death of Christ gained its power to satisfy the injured dignity of God and so acquire merit because it was the only possible way or was only one of many ways that God chose to accept. Obviously this question is too recondite to interest the non-theological mind. It was very much simpler to say that by the sacrifice of Calvary and the mass God was placated, that is to say, any obstacle to the exercise of God's love was removed by Jesus' death. But it would be a mistake to think that the scholastic theology made such a use of the death of Christ the center of its doctrine as to salvation. That lay rather in the center of Christianity itself, actual transformation of human nature by the grace of God manifested by the sacraments as well as through faith. The theologian might have his problems within what might be called a philosophy as to the death of Christ, but the great mass of Christians were not called upon to accept any of these philosophies as final. They had the mass and the sacrament, and the experience of grace. Their fears of punishment for original and actual sin were removed by the transfer to them of the merit acquired by Jesus by his incomparable suffering and death. That simpler belief in the supremacy of the love of God which, as has already been said, occasionally appeared in the Schoolmen, never by itself became a basis for Christian hope. The pardoning love of God had in some way to be found rooted in a motive other than itself and justified by the use of the death of Christ. The difficulties which lay in a current pardoning of criminals and rebels, with the means by which these difficulties were resolved became a pattern by which the message of forgiveness and the confidence in the means of grace were justified.

Medieval Christianity was thus developing in two directions: on the one side there was the religious technique which had become organized in the experience of centuries and found expression in the actual practice of the church, and on the other hand was the speculative interest of the theological literati which sought to rationalize those practices by showing them to be congruous with unquestioned assumptions springing from scientific and philosophical presuppositions and social practices. It was not until Protestantism abandoned the priesthood and the transsubstantiation as the explanation of the real presence of Christ in the elements of the Lord's Supper that atonement by the death of Christ became important for the mass of church members. Then it was that theological orthodoxy in a large measure came in Protestantism to play the rôle played in Catholicism by church rites and discipline.

CHAPTER IX

THE DEATH OF CHRIST IN THE PATTERN OF MONARCHY

HISTORY is not laid out in chronological lots in which one epoch ends as another begins. Rather, history is like the growth of an organism in which there is differentiation of new organs but also the survival of the old. A reform is seldom able to bring about the absolute destruction of that which it attacks; it usually produces some new social custom or institution while elements of the older situation continue. For this reason the sharp distinction between the Reformation from the Renaissance is artificial. New conditions did arise, but old conditions, more or less modified, continued. The Roman Church with its inherited imperialism was not destroyed, but in certain countries it was replaced by religious groups which had broken away from its control. But within the area of the old Roman Empire the Protestant movement was never successful. The world which Rome created remained loyal to its ancestor.

Among the peoples that hung on the northern flank of the Roman Empire the influence of Rome was by no means great. These northern tribes had become Christian more or less under compulsion, and they had no choice but to accept the organization of the Catholic Church. Even when they moved to England and confronted the British church and felt the influence of the Irish missionaries, these peoples were under the ecclesiastical control of the *curia.* But this ecclesiastical unity was not rooted in a history and a civilization as in France, Spain, and Italy. To the feudal states of Germany with their uneasily seated kings and their traditional emperor, Rome was a foreign authority. Their religion might make these German states the fellows of other states, but their only political unity was in the Diet of the Empire over which a Hapsburg had come to preside as emperor. Theoretically this Diet would be expected to carry out its duties as conceived in the theory of the Holy Roman Empire. This would mean that it would be expected to carry on such political and military action as would be involved in the policy of the Pope. With this relationship of the small German states with Rome through the Diet the German nobles had always been more or less impatient. From the days of Henry IV German politics had involved contests with the Pope.

The Reformation was, in fact, one of the long series of struggles between German political units and the Roman *curia.* Its origins lie quite as much in an inherited psychology as in any of its more dramatic occasions. A nation, like some people, has long memories and hereditary feuds.

I

It is impossible to understand the Reformation movement if attention be centered on Germany. Luther's career really dramatized a new social mind which found expression over all western Europe, in France and Spain as truly as in England and Saxony. The reason that it had such different outcomes is complicated but largely attributable to the difference already noticed between the situation within and without the old Roman Empire. Whatever these differences were, the creative forces were marked largely by the same economic, social, and political characteristics. It would have been contrary to all human experience if these forces had not expressed themselves in the field of religion as well as in that of politics. It would have been also quite contrary to our knowledge of human nature if the institutions represented in the older situation had not vigorously opposed changes which the new social forces involved. Here again we see a difference between the Roman and the extra-Roman countries. In the former creative forces found cultural and political expression, but the religious status after the evolution remained unchanged. In the latter regions the political development was involved in the religious, and there came far more marked changes in the religious than in the political situation.

These creative forces can in a general way be described as the development of the modern state with its monarchy, its laws, and its public officials. In it every individual is a subject of the monarch and obedient to his laws. It is true that in Europe the feudal relations continued in local relations particularly of the peasantry, and to some extent in the relations of the feudal houses, but their end was in sight when the power of the king became greater than the power of the feudal lord. The political transformation through which Spain, France, and England passed in the fourteenth, fifteenth, and sixteenth centuries, inaugurated a new epoch. Furthermore, although, possibly because of the Empire, the same national unity did not result in Germany, the new idea of sovereignty, law, and political relations appeared in more or less modified form in the German states.

New economic conditions stimulated and indeed, necessitated this change in political structure. Important as feudalism had been as a first step in the reestablishing of order in a disintegrated world, its own lack of unity and the non-participation of the feudal classes in economic life made anything like progressive economic development impossible. It was only when the cities gained power and great feudal states began to emerge from feudal atomism that commerce and various industries were free to develop. The vast increase of silver which followed the discovery of America caused a rise in prices which not only stimulated trade but undermined feudal superiority and necessitated the sort of legislation that only a centralized government could enforce. The knights found themselves caught between rising towns and the expansion of the great fiefs. Economic distress waited for them. In consequence they not only felt that the Roman church with its enormous economic privileges and power was largely responsible for their misfortune, but they also felt the inadequacy of the old feudal structure. For them freedom meant some sort of nationalism to oppose situations which they were beginning to find intolerable. It was natural, therefore, that like their opponents in the cities and the business world they should welcome legal uniformity enforced by a central authority.

Thus a new and creative spirit was coming over all western Europe. New political institutions arose in which sovereignty and law were two foci of politics, and punishment in the name of the sovereign and the law was that upon which social order had to rely. As in feudalism the political structure could not endure if the lower classes ceased to recognize the larger honor of the higher and the higher could not enforce satisfaction for injury to their honor, so in the sixteenth and seventeenth centuries no government could be thought of as maintaining itself if the sovereign lost his power to enforce his laws by punishment. Jurisprudence was imperfectly developed; the old Roman law was not established in the political life, but one thing was clear—the social order depended upon sovereignty and sovereignty depended upon the ability of the sovereign to maintain respect for his laws by punishing their violation. Justice became thus identified with punishment. Laws were to be enforced by fear of punishment, and Europe was dotted with gallows. If punishment were not inflicted upon those who disobeyed the king's law, the king's own sovereignty would be endangered. The pardoning of criminals was thus dangerous because on the one side it might indicate that the sovereign had lost his authority and power, while on the other side it might argue that the sovereign had no regard for his law and was thus undermining his own authority.

This authority which rested upon its own self found expression in the field of theology. Just as the political and juridical system became more unified did the theological system become more sharply political. What the theologians came to call the punitive justice of God, became his fundamental characteristic. His love was to be squared by proper relationship to this punitive justice exactly as Anselm had squared the divine love with the satisfaction of the injured dignity of God. The political literature of the time makes it evident that the absoluteness of the sovereign was unquestioned. It became an unconsciously held presupposition of thought and conduct. Political practices and conceptions about which there was no question became the pattern for theological thought. God had always been regarded as a sovereign, but now he became thought of as the new type of sovereign whose very position depended upon the maintenance of his punitive power. If he did not maintain this punitive power, the moral order as well as his own position was endangered. Biblical expressions were freely given this new political content and the picture of God as the king among the Hebrews was filled in with the practices of the kings of the sixteenth and seventeenth centuries. In many respects the two conceptions were at one, but with the rise of Protestantism, the biblical concept was expanded by appeal to social practices and ideas that were not to be found in the political structures of the biblical period. Punishment had been delegated to devils and hell was their place of torment.

The basic issue between the Protestant movement and the Roman Catholic in the sixteenth century was centered around the juridical idea of acquittal by which one escaped hell and gained heaven at the coming judgment. This justification of man by a sovereign God was said by the Protestants to depend only on faith, while the Catholics insisted that it depended upon faith and works. In both cases, justification was the removal of the guilt which came from original and actual sin. In the case of the Protestants it had no moral content whatever. The possibility of a person's being thus acquitted at the Judgment Day, and even his power to have faith were conditioned upon the sovereign act of God who elected him from the mass of a humanity doomed to eternal punishment because of the sin of Adam. An intense desire to escape punishment in hell must be borne in mind if the theological discussions of the centuries are to be understood. All parties would agree in the broad lines of what salvation involved, both in the enjoyment of heaven and in "sanctification" in the earthly life. The great question in their minds concerned God's acquittal of sinners who deserved such favor no more than the rest of the race.

Both Roman Catholic and Protestant theologians began with the assumption of Augustine's doctrine of original sin, but in the new epoch the emphasis of exposition passed from the corruption of nature to the guilt of the human race. Calvin, with his legally trained mind, thoroughly systematized this conception, but it is quite as fundamental with Luther. All individual human beings were guilty because they partook of a human nature that had sinned in Adam. Occasionally this guilt of the individual was raised to terrible distinctness and the individual himself was held to be responsible for Adam's sin. Even when, under the stress of later constitutional habits the pattern was changed so that Adam became the representative of the human race, guilt was uppermost in theological thought. The process of salvation was thus clearly stated. Men must be relieved from their guilt, else all the good works they might do were worse than worthless. From this point of view of guilt as distinct from moral quality, much of the theological thought, especially the preaching with which the Protestants have assailed the so-called moral man, is intelligible. So long as a man in the status of the rebel is liable to punishment, any good deed that he performs serves only to blind him to his perilous position. It is as if a man under sentence of death could believe that he was to escape because he had given a present to the child of a beggar. The political pattern seemed axiomatic. God was a sovereign, punishment must follow violation of the law. Hell waited for the guilty race as the gallows waited for the criminal. If God wished to forgive he must in some way satisfy his justice.

Theological teaching cannot be fully understood simply by the study of the works of theologians. One needs to go to sermons and attempts of the clergy to induce men actually to adopt religious practices if one is to understand theology, for theology is in its origin practical and dramatically metaphorical. The frequent use of such metaphors tends to deprive them of their metaphorical quality and make them unquestioned patterns for the control of thought. So it was in the case of the use of sovereignty and the political practices and preconceptions of the days when absolute monarchy was replacing feudalism. It seemed to men who were experiencing the relentless and doubtless indispensable justice of their monarchs that God himself must give attention first of all to the maintenance of his sovereignty by seeing to it that guilty human nature should not escape punishment. Anselm no more demanded satisfaction of God's dignity than the theologians of the Reformation period assumed the need of satisfying

God's punitive justice. They passed from the scholastic realism of human nature to the corollary of sovereignty that each individual must have his guilt removed before he could hope for moral change. Guilt, however, could be removed only by punishment or by pardon. But pardon was impossible unless punishment had been inflicted.

So far there is no real difference between the theologians of historic Christianity, whether it be Roman Catholic or Lutheran or Calvinist. All of men's relations with God are included within the framework of a transcendentalized state whose characteristics are those of contemporary political institutions. Under the domination of these political concepts all theologians were agreed that the death of Christ had in some way met the conditions and had so far satisfied the justice of God as to leave him free to pardon those whom he would. Differences, however, arose in the extension of this central pattern. On the one side the Roman Catholic did not feel any great need of raising into theological importance any view of the significance of the death of Jesus, which was not already involved in his sacrifice and his satisfaction of divine dignity. Their expositions and discussions do, indeed, speak of his justice and they are not opposed to the pattern which became so central in Protestant thought. But there really was no need on the part of the masses for any particular attention on the part of the Roman clergy to a doctrine of the atonement. Justification was not dependent upon faith alone and could be dramatically as well as intellectually mediated to the masses. On the other hand, it was of the utmost importance for the Protestants to organize their conception of the death of Christ as a dogma. The removal of guilt was possible in the case of those who had faith in him.

II

In the voluminous literature which Luther has left us there is considerable variety of exposition in all fields of theology and, rather strangely, there are almost irreconcilable expressions relative to faith. Melanchthon, with his systematic mind, has no hesitation in equating the faith of which Paul speaks with trust (*fiducia*).[1] Luther, however, sometimes speaks of faith in the sense of trust and sometimes in the sense of belief which has definite intellectual content. While any general statement would be subject to exception, it would seem as if he used the word in the former sense when he was addressing Christians and showing them the way to that assurance of salvation which is his substitute for reliance upon the authority of the church. One can be sure that one is to be justified because one has the belief that he is to be justified.[2] It was this particular basis of Christian assurance that the Council of Trent expressly condemned.[3] It was

[1] Frank, *op. cit.*, I, 407.
[2] Augsburg Confession, art. 4.
[3] Decrees of Council of Trent.

consistent in so doing. At least in his earlier days, before Luther was forced to defend and express the corporate attitudes of a newly organized church, the great reformer was singularly reliant upon Christian experience as its own best evidence. Trust in God's mercy was regarded as the expression of that newness of life which argued the favor of God.

But there is the other Luther who undertook to set forth in explicit fashion the intellectual content of this assurance that a man was forgiven when he believed that God for Christ's sake had forgiven him. Such a belief was more than a psychological drama. It included the acceptance of the "Gospel." In the early stages of the Lutheran movement the gospel is used where later theologians would have used the word "Bible," and the transition from the one to the other has real significance. It is one thing to believe the good news of God's forgiveness and another thing to ground one's theological system on a literature that has been given authority not only in the realm of saving truth but in history, science, and all other matters which it touches. When the new reformation organized its beliefs for the benefit of the princes who in the Diet of Augsburg in 1530 wished to explain to Charles V just what their position was, the chief importance seemed to be not so much theological precision as exposition of just how the Protestant movement differed from the great religious system from which it was separating. But sooner or later one was bound to ask just what the gospel is and where it could be found. In considering this matter the party of Luther showed clearly how they carried forward the continuity of Christian history. At first the gospel is found epitomized in the Apostles', Nicene, and Athanasian creeds, but by 1576, when the divergent Lutheran groups found a basis of concord, there was added the unchanged Augsburg Confession, with the Apology, the Smalcald Articles, and the Smaller and Larger Catechisms of Luther. By this time the concept of the gospel had been largely replaced by a general theological system, and faith had thus become ecclesiastical rather than psychological. While, indeed, there are certain expressions which Luther himself used which would seem to imply that he believed that correct theological belief, even Lutheranism itself, was necessary for salvation,[4] it is clear that the importance of these elements of faith increased as the movement he inaugurated developed, gained ecclesiastical structure and needed theological precision. Certainly he would never have thought that any assurance would be possible to a man who was not a believer in the deity of Christ and the Trinity. Anything less than this would in his opinion have been an indication of an unsaved condition.

[4] See Rashdall, *op. cit.*, p. 414. It would seem, however, that Rashdall has rather overstated the case when he says (p. 409) that faith to Luther is simply belief. The double usage of the term seems to me more likely, the emphasis being set by the particular object which Luther at the moment had in mind. The psychology of theological argument and pastoral encouragement is different, and the consequent exposition of the same idea may also vary.

Furthermore, there naturally developed the necessity of giving some intellectual content to the statement that God for Christ's sake had forgiven men. It is here that the political pattern becomes a dominant characteristic of the Lutheran thought. The death of Christ is still spoken of as a sacrifice and he is said to have given satisfaction to God, but when this is expounded, the creative social mind which was remaking the politics of Europe finds expression. It is punishment which Christ bears, not merely suffering. The homiletic vigor of Luther dramatized this punitive experience of Christ extravagantly. He is said to have become the sinner and to have been made an actual substitute for sinners. "All the prophets," Luther declares,[5] "saw this in spirit, that Christ would be of all men the greatest robber, homicide, adulterer, thief, doer of sacrilege, blasphemer, etc., that ever was in the world, because, as a victim for the sins of the whole world, he is not an innocent person and without sins."

But it would hardly be fair to do more than treat this as an illustration of that vigorous rhetoric which preachers have always felt justified in using. Probably Luther would have been the last man to say that such expressions were meant to be taken literally. But in them as in subsequent Protestant thought, the idea of substitution in the actual suffering of punishment becomes essential to the doctrine of the atonement. The practice of sacrifice had so completely disappeared from

[5] Commentary on Galatians, ch. 3.

social usages that it could be explained only by reference to the Hebrew ritual as a sort of type. The ransom to Satan would be particularly unpalatable for the Protestant theologian, because of its close kinship with the rejected belief in purgatory. Dignity and honor still had social values and were used in theology, but the really creative concept was that of the satisfaction of the punitive justice of a sovereign God. In that sense Jesus was the lamb of God, the sacrificial and the juridical concepts being confused.

But there remained the question how the punitive sufferings of Jesus which the transcendentalized politics demanded could be transferred to the benefit of the believer. The answer to such a question was drawn unexpectedly from the conception of merit which had become an unquestioned part of the Catholic system of thought. For the Protestant as well as the Roman Catholic merit could be transferred from one who did not need it to one who otherwise would have been lost without it. The differences between the Protestant and the Catholic at this point were twofold. On the one side the Protestant denied that there were merits gained by saints, the transfer of which could benefit other men, and they also believed that the transfer of merit was conditioned wholly upon faith. The central idea, however, was the same in both systems. Jesus in enduring punishment had done that which he was under no moral obligation to do, and therefore had acquired merit which could be imputed to those who believed that God for Christ's sake had forgiven them.

Another element, however, appears at this point in the Protestant thought. It was not only the merit of Christ but his righteousness, his active obedience, which could be used in satisfying the requirements of divine justice. This righteousness, as well as his merit, could be imputed to the believer. The idea of imputation of the merits and righteousness of Christ by God is the Protestant equivalent of the Catholic power of binding and loosing and the control of the treasury of merit. The Protestants were apparently forced into such a position by the exigencies of their theological struggle. In the Augsburg Confession the formula is strictly Pauline. It is men's faith that is imputed for righteousness, that is to say, non-liability to punishment. By the time of the Formula of Concord, however, it is the merits and righteousness of Christ that are imputed, a doctrine which has no sound biblical basis and is really a survival of the ecclesiastical history from which Protestantism sprang.[6]

III

This political character of doctrine appears even more distinctly in the Calvinist theology. Its entire system centers around the conception of God as sovereign, "to whose will the desire of kings ought to be subject, to whose decrees all their commands ought to

[6] Formula of Concord, art. iii.

submit."[7] God "rules by fixed decrees." He is the celestial Judge[8] before whom all men are to appear for judgment. All the other elements of the Calvinist system are corollaries of this central doctrine. Nor is this strange. Calvin, trained as a lawyer, was possessed of a very different temperament from Luther, and Calvinism is more thoroughly and systematically developed than is Lutheranism. In both alike there is found a constant emphasis upon faith, and in the *Institutes* Calvin appeals far more to Christian experience than popular belief would probably hold. But Calvinism as a system is closed. At certain points it has been softened but only at the expense of its logic. The whole process of Christian redemption rested upon a decree of God. Humanity was to be restored to fellowship with God by some mediator who was without sin. He must needs be God and man. Humanity in him was to be given value by the presence of the divine, therefore the incarnation. Calvin meets the Roman priesthood by insisting[9] that the Christ was prophet, king, and priest. As priest he could be a basis of reconciliation between man and God. The basis of this reconciliation is not exclusively the death of Christ, but his entire life. "He purchased a righteousness which made God favorable and kind to us . . . by the whole course

[7] *Institutes of the Christian Religion,* bk. iv, 32. For a full discussion see bk. i, ch. 16. There the government of God is said to be extended to all His works; "the faithful suffer no affliction but by the ordination and command of God."

[8] *Institutes,* bk. iii, 1.

[9] *Institutes,* bk. ii, ch. 15.

of his obedience." That is to say, his entire life had reconciling significance but it was his death particularly that was effective. Jesus Christ was condemned to death though innocent. "He put on the character of Adam, and assumed his name, to act as his substitute in his obedience to the Father, to lay down our flesh as the price of satisfaction to the justice of God; and to suffer the punishment which we have deserved."[10] He offered up his flesh "in order to expiate and obliterate our guilt, and appease the just wrath of the Father." And all this was by "the eternal decree of God." On Jesus alone men must fix their eyes and hearts, since it is by him alone that they really obtain the non-imputation of sins, the imputation of which is connected with the divine wrath.[11] But Christ's death was a part of his entire obedience and because of it "he continually appears in the presence of the Father as our advocate and intercessor; he attracts the eyes of the Father to his righteousness, so as to avert them from our sins; he reconciles him to us, so as to procure for us, by his intercession, a way of access to his throne."[12] Human guilt was transferred to him and as our substitute he bore the curse that had been laid upon humanity.[13] Guilt therefore cannot be imputed to the elect. A man is justified by faith when "he lays hold

[10] *Institutes,* bk. ii, ch. 12, 3, cf. ch. 16, 2.

[11] *Institutes,* bk. ii, ch. 16, 3.

[12] *Institutes,* bk. ii, ch. 16, 16. In ch. 17 Calvin shows how Christ merited the grace of God and salvation for us.

[13] *Institutes,* bk. ii, ch. 16, 3.

of the righteousness of Christ, and, clothed in it, appears in the sight of God not as a sinner but as righteous." Justification is the "imputation of the righteousness of Christ" and the Christian is "clothed" with it. In this position the two streams of Protestantism united, faith being the sole basis of the divine acquittal, and moral graces following rather than accompanying the act of faith. In neither branch of the older Protestantism was justification considered other than forensic. Christian experience rather than justification involved the conception of process.[14] The pattern of absolute sovereignty with decrees and unconditioned acts control Protestant as well as Roman theology. It is the center of the theology of all the reformed Confessions. To affirm any moral power on the part of humanity or to hold that men could by moral act in any way share in the work of their own justification was regarded as heresy.

IV

The political pattern is somewhat modified in the federal theology in which the relations of God and man are set forth in terms of covenants made by God with mankind. Of these there were two, first the covenant of works made with Adam as the representative of the human race, which was annulled by the fall. It was to

[14] Luther, it is true, does occasionally speak of justification in terms that would indicate process, but only when it would appear that his thought was centered upon salvation rather than upon justification itself.

the effect that if Adam kept the law he would enjoy divine favor, again as representative of the human race. As he did not obey God, divine love led to the establishment of the covenant of grace according to which God treated Christ as the representative of the elect, and those who joined him shared in the blessings which belonged to the obedient. That is to say, Christ in this transaction represented the elect.[15]

It would be a nice question in historical criticism to discover the precise relations of this covenant theology with the contract philosophy of government which was to play such a revolutionary rôle in the politics of the eighteenth century. Obviously it is to some extent a modification of the absolute sovereignty of God, for his covenant set certain limitations upon his action. In this regard it was in a way a faint prophecy of the constitutional monarchy, one essential element of which was the limitation of the existing sovereignty by the agreement of the sovereign. Furthermore, this theology carries within itself that conception of the relations of the sovereign and his people which were to be so extensively developed by Rousseau. But it is a fair question whether the theology or the political philosophy was first. When one recalls the important rôle which Hooker's *Ecclesiastical Polity* played in the development of the theory of the social contract, it is not diffi-

[15] These conceptions occur in all the more important Calvinist confessions.

cult to believe that the federal theology, which rested so thoroughly on the interpretation of scripture, was a cause quite as much as an effect of the political theory. But it is also noticeable that this type of theology was never popular in countries where the idea of constitutional government was absent. In Holland it became a source of ecclesiastical dispute, and in New England it became one of the important elements of theological thought. It is not surprising that the Roman church in the Council of Trent should have condemned it. The attitude of mind which could find satisfaction in the type of government represented by constitutions and compacts would never be satisfied with the absolutism of the Roman *curia.*

The representative quality of both Adam and Jesus is an indication of the new social mind which in the seventeenth century was developing the formulas of democracy. Such representation was, of course, far enough from being strictly democratic, for neither had the race elected Adam nor the elect selected Christ as their representative. To this extent, therefore, it would be quite impossible to regard the federal theology as an expression of democracy, and yet in a sense the democratic element is implied in that the believer is enabled to regard Christ as his representative, and thus to take advantage of the fact that Christ had borne the punishment of the elect. Reference to the debt owed by humanity to God belongs to the general circle of political rather than of economic experience, for the right to punish the debtor was in the seventeenth century a recognized power of the state.

V

Socinus indistinctly appreciated this fact. He was convinced that the real meaning of the death of Christ was not that of penal suffering. God has a perfect right to forgive without requiring any satisfaction. His righteousness is something more than punitive justice and his love is not under the control of his justice. Yet evidently Socinus had not really broken with the political pattern in his thought of God. He is thinking in accordance with that pattern when he goes on to argue that satisfaction is not necessary and righteousness cannot be imputed. In such arguments there is no change in the conception of God and the entire relationship of man and God is argued from the commonly accepted theology. Christ did expiate the sins of the world, and he continually intercedes with God and frees us from our sins. He is a priest, but the chief value of his death according to Socinus is so close to the Pauline view as to be unacceptable to the champion of the highly developed theological system of the sixteenth century. "Jesus Christ is our savior because he proclaimed to us the way of eternal life, confirmed it, and clearly showed it forth both by the example of his life and by rising again from the dead, and because he will give eternal life to us who have faith in him." [16] Thus in the Socinian system there appears a distrust of the political pattern yet no substitute for it. Emphasizing though it does the moral aspects of the work of Christ, its moral conceptions themselves involve the power of the sovereign and the obligations of the subject. The difference between the sovereign God of Socinus and the sovereign God of Calvin is chiefly that between academic benevolence and effective administration. This may be the reason why the morally more perplexing conception of God in Calvinism has prevailed. If men are to have a sovereign God they want one who does express his sovereignty.

VI

It may have been this sort of conviction that accounts for the criticism of Grotius upon the thought of Socinus. The historical student is much more concerned with Grotius as the father of international law than as the author of a theory of the death of Christ that attempted to correct the views of Socinus and at the same time avoid the disagreeable elements of scholastic Protestantism. As we look back upon his period now, it is not difficult to see how a man deeply interested in law should have endeavored to find something in theology more fundamental than the relations of subject to mon-

[16] *De Jesu Christu Servatori.* Quoted by Mosely, *Doctrine of the Atonement,* p. 150.

arch. Some conception was needed that would also recognize the relation of nations to nations. This Grotius found in the supremacy of law, which was something more than the promulgations of a sovereign, in fact was superior to sovereignty itself. Whereas the government of an individual state might by punishment enforce its laws, it was itself subject to the higher obligation of maintaining the dignity of law itself, and this sovereign law would hold in the relations of nations when once they, too, came to realize that such relations were something more than conditions which could be determined by conquest.

This political philosophy Grotius applied to the exposition of the death of Christ. He broke with the Socinians in insisting that the death of Christ did have a value Godward and with the orthodox Protestants by insisting that God was the governor rather than the feudal lord or judge. Punishment for sin fell upon Christ not because he was the substitute for the sinful race but because it was necessary that the law which had been violated by humanity should be vindicated by the infliction of punishment. There was danger lest the forgiveness of sinners might lead others to the contempt of divine law. The suffering of Christ is not quantitatively viewed, but is supposed to be sufficient to show the immutability of law.

Here we see a fundamental shift in the significance of the sufferings of Christ. In the case of Anselm and the orthodox Catholic or Protestant, the death of Christ has a bearing upon God in meeting some demand in his own being. With Grotius, however, one might say it respects public opinion as represented by sinful humanity. The death of Jesus as a vindication of the sovereignty of law rather curiously becomes a means for deterring sinners from wrongdoing and especially from condemning God as the moral governor of the universe. There could hardly be a better illustration of the danger that lies in any attempt to analyze a pattern and to develop its corollaries. And even this disclosure cannot obscure the tendency of thinkers to express the significance of the death of Christ in patterns which represent dominant elements of their own experience. It is only when one raises the question as to whether God actually is a sovereign that its analogical meaning becomes apparent. And if God be not a sovereign in a literal sense, then all the implications as to the need of satisfying his punitive justice or his honor, or showing the sovereignty of his law suddenly vanish. If God be thought of as father such corollaries could not be drawn. If he is to be thought of from the point of view of cosmic process they disappear still further into intellectual space. One cannot think of a cosmic God as possessing qualities of a sixteenth-century sovereign. In other words, the meaning of the death of Christ is determined by one's conception of God.

VII

How far removed from a present interest in religion are the questions raised by political patterns in theology appears from a consideration of the struggle between the thorough-going Calvinist and the Arminians which culminated in the Synod of Dort (1619). The chief difference between the Arminians and the Calvinists had to do with predestination and its implications. The Arminian view began with the premise of the sovereignty of God and attempted to adjust that sovereignty to man's freedom. It was perhaps as successful as any solution of such a question may hope to be, but it is difficult to see how it can be more than emotional and literary. The Calvinist, on the contrary, was consistent logically. If the sovereignty of God be absolute, it is hard to see how it can be modified by human or other causes. Ecumenical Calvinism as represented in the Synod of Dort could hardly do other than take the position in its famous five points. If one's human nature is regarded as unable to choose the right because of original sin, as orthodoxy, whether Calvinist or Lutheran, claimed, it is difficult to see how the death of Christ should not be logically limited to the elect, or how the elect could withstand the grace of God or how they could ever fall from that grace. The Arminians modified the strict implications of absolute sovereignty by the human consciousness of choice and saw in the fallen nature of man at least traces of an original righteousness. One can thus hold to the universality of atonement, man's ability to reject grace, and the possibility of falling from grace.

But here again theological difficulties really result from the pattern in which God's relations with men are expressed. If that pattern be abandoned the questions raised by Arminianism do not appear. Other and very serious questions emerge, but they spring from the other patterns. One could not, for example, think of affirming or denying that Cosmic Activity issues decrees, or exercises prevenient and irresistible grace. The values that these patterns properly interpreted may express continue, but the particular theological difficulties disappear. And with the abandonment of the political pattern there disappears also the guilt of humanity which deserves punishment. The empirical facts which, from the days of Augustine on, were used as evidence of guilt may remain but they are given another setting. From the point of view of evolution there can be no universal fall of humanity from a stage of moral innocence nor a discovery of sin in sex. The entire conception of sin is radically changed. With these theological patterns go all doctrines of the atonement drawn from them. They, too, become analogies rather than facts.

Satisfaction of the divine honor, endurance of penal sufferings to satisfy divine justice, the imputation of righteousness to persons elected from a morally impotent race, the fires of hell and the golden streets of Jerusalem are patterns in which the ultimate relations of men and God can be described. So viewed, they are no more literal than the music of the spheres and the breath of spring. But methodically examined they are seen to express religious attitudes and values which constitute the very heart of the Christian's faith. And this faith he is already beginning to legitimatize by patterns drawn from natural sciences and social experience of our modern world.

CHAPTER X

MODIFICATIONS OF THE POLITICAL PATTERN

A STRUGGLE between absolute sovereignty and the political right of the individual to have a share in the making of laws, the levying of taxes, the waging of war, and the control of the police power, the substitution of economic for feudal relations in land-owning, and the elimination of different grades of honor were the creative interests of the seventeenth and eighteenth centuries. In the seventeenth century this conflict brought about the fall of the Stuarts and the supremacy of Parliament, and in the eighteenth century produced the republic of the United States of America and the French Revolution. Such far-spreading changes were due in large measure to the rise of the middle, that is to say the commercial class, who never had any feudal status but who had greatly developed economically through commerce and in the latter part of the period through industry. The rise of capital was accompanied by the wage system which for a century or more put the employer in much the same position of control over workmen as had formerly been enjoyed by the feudal lord. With the rise of economic power there came naturally the determination to gain political authority.

The rising *bourgeoisie* was the inevitable and implacable enemy of feudal privilege and absolute monarchy. Each party to the struggle sought the defeat of the others and each sought the control of wealth and the power to enforce law by punishment.

I

This hostility to absolutism resulted in the transfer of certain of the prerogatives of the English monarchy to Parliament, and the English royalty found itself controlled by the Act of Settlement and the Bill of Rights. Other nations of the world were to postpone the struggle for a century or more but there came into English life a new basic conception as to the position of the sovereign and the entire structure of the state.

This change of political theory found expression theologically in the movement commonly called deism. Whatever may have been its philosophical basis and exposition, its true nature was akin to that which was taking place in the constitutional history of the nation. As the power of the Stuarts was transferred to Parliament and the royal house decreasingly controlled political forces and national resources, so the God of Calvinism was pictured as abandoning certain of his prerogatives in the interest of nature. Scientific thought was yet very incomplete, but the struggle between a theology that was a transcendentalized political absolutism and an understanding of the forces of the universe was beginning. Deism was in fact the counterpart in religion of the English revolution in politics. The truth of this appears when one compares the French with the English philosophical development of the seventeenth and eighteenth centuries. Deism in so far as it utilized the political pattern could be significant only among a people accustomed to constitutional government. When it passed to France where constitutional government did not exist it became a philosophical atheism. There was no political pattern to intervene between the absolute sovereignty of God and no God whatever. Atheism in this regard was logically more tenable than deism, for a sovereign God exercising his power under constitutional limitations set by natural law is obviously a God rapidly becoming emeritus.

It would not be fair, however, to the Deists to say that they consciously elaborated any parallelism between their philosophy and their politics. They regarded themselves as working scientifically from the point of view of natural religion, that is to say, those religious beliefs which were innate in the very nature of man. Without any real knowledge of the other religions of the world they found a so-called natural religion by removing from Christianity its peculiarly historical element. It would be difficult to find any modern student of the history of religion who would claim that a belief in a single supreme God who was to be worshiped by piety and virtue, who forgives a sinner if only he repent, is to be found in primitive religion. The explanation of natural religion was, however, to have one very important influence. It marked the beginning of a substitution of the scientific for the political criteria of faith. If there were a natural religion it might be held by those who found it impossible to accept the theology of scholastic Protestantism. Christianity would be regarded skeptically, while the tenets of natural religion would be held. Indeed the very conception of a natural religion would sooner or later begin to undermine the entire structure which orthodoxy had built upon the death of Christ as required by the demands of a divine sovereignty. A really significant thinker like Locke pointed out how far apart the natural religion demonstrable by reason was from the elements of Christianity given by revelation. Whether a given doctrine was the result of revelation would depend upon whether it actually came from God. To introduce this question was clearly to introduce a question as to the Bible itself. Locke stripped away views which had accumulated about the fall, and stated sharply the long-since-abandoned Pauline view that death rather than guilt was the outcome of Adam's disobedience. This death passed on to his descendants. Men can be delivered from this death by faith in Jesus as the Messiah. This is the law of faith which replaces the law of works. But at this point Locke could not free himself from the current pattern and thought of Christ as king. His honor and the kingdom over which he ruled was given him by God as a reward for his having died for others.

The subjects of this kingdom were those who had faith in the king. But when philosophy undertook to set forth the significance of the kingship of Jesus, it became evident that the political pattern is no longer axiomatic, for the real work of the historical Jesus, Locke held, was that of revelation, supplementing the evidence of God in nature. He was also the teacher of morality, the reformer of the Hebrew religion, the teacher of the spiritual nature of kinship, and instigator of the new moral life based upon the gift of the Holy Spirit.

Such a view, dominated as it is by a philosophy of religion rather than the documents and confessions of Protestantism, is the first step toward the abandonment of the political pattern as essential to an understanding of the work of Christ. In such a scheme of thought there is no room for punitive justice or penal suffering. All those passages of the New Testament which were used by the orthodox theologians as proof texts for such views are treated by Locke either allegorically or as metaphorical. In this he anticipated the historical method of later days. Indeed, the entire movement of deism was in the direction of historical criticism and the use of the New Testament as historical material rather than as theological oracle. The historical sciences, to say nothing of the natural sciences, were not sufficiently developed to give a distinct methodology, but the abandonment of the primacy of the political conception in theology is clearly prophesied. As long as the idea of guilt in the legal sense prevailed it would give color to any interpretation given the significance of the death of Christ. When the forensic pattern was abandoned, as in the case of certain Deists, there was the frank rejection of the Hebrew conception of God as an absolute sovereign making "mere capricious humor and arbitrary will the rule and measure of his actions in his dealings with mankind." On the contrary, God "makes the eternal rule of right and wrong the measure of his actions." [1] It is little wonder that the orthodox theologians of the eighteenth century should have regarded deism as tantamount to atheism, for there was substituted for the infallible Bible the rule of reason.[2]

As often happens in theological controversy, the points of discussion were set by the heretic. The representatives of the church doctrine were thrown on the defensive. As a result, the discussion centered around philosophical and exegetical issues. Both deists and theists started with the anthropomorphic conception of God. He was the sovereign, who either had or had not transferred his prerogatives to nature. This presupposition appears in an opponent of deism like Bishop Butler, whose *Analogy* is a theological classic. To him revealed religion included the natural, and he attempted to find in nature analogies to revealed religion. But

[1] Quoted by Frank, *The Work of Christ,* p. 173.

[2] Edwards, *Works,* I, 467. "The Deists wholly cast off the Christian religion and are professed infidels.

to our modern world, artificial, method of Butler was an apologetic weapon to be grasped only by the clergy and philosophers. The social mind that could really create the axioms of constructive thought was political and economic. The philosophical movement of the Illumination had indeed its influence, but it was relatively narrow and negative. The French and English philosophical thought of the eighteenth century had not yet received from Kant a discipline in critical thought, and had too much self-confidence to realize that brilliant writing is not necessarily truth.

II

But the Illumination itself was really the intellectual penumbra of profound social change. Although the men of the middle of the eighteenth century were to die without seeing the fulfillment of their promises, feudalism and absolute sovereignty were really hastening to their end. But they were slain not by "natural" men, but by the trader, the banker, the farmer, the wage earner, who proved that the philosophers were right in saying that sovereignty resided in the people. Democracy and the capital-wage system were really two aspects of the same profound change which marked the beginning of our modern social order.

How government came to exist, what rights the sovereign had, how far the people could replevy natural rights taken from them by the sovereign, how sovereignty could be transferred to the people, how government could aid industry and commerce, how and by whom taxes should be levied, how debts could be collected and wealth accumulated—these were the really creative interests of Europe and America. But until the middle of the nineteenth century such interests led to economic and political reconstruction only in England, the United States, and France.

So far as strictly theological thought of the eighteenth century is concerned, France can be neglected. There was philosophical thought in France but it was negative and on the whole antagonistic to religion. In England the Wesleyan and Baptist movements were not primarily theological in character, although the former was tinged with Arminianism and the latter was sturdily Calvinist. But neither movement gave rise to any new theological system or pattern. The Wesleyan movement took over the majority of the Thirty-nine Articles and the Baptist accepted a modified Westminster Confession. The simple fact seems to be that orthodoxy of the later eighteenth and the early nineteenth centuries found it impossible to exploit further the political pattern and the corollaries of sovereignty. It unconsciously shrank from the logical rigor of the seventeenth century, especially as regards the extent of the atonement. Beneath the surface of the Calvinist thought new economic and political forces were weakening those axiomatic presuppositions which had been so theologically fertile a hundred years before.

This new though tentative situation was to find its most influential expression in the American theologian, Jonathan Edwards.[3] Living as he did in the last days of an absolute Protestant orthodoxy, his philosophical interest centered largely around conditions set by the sovereignty of God. His Calvinism was thorough-going, as his discussions of sin and the state of the non-elect go to show. The work of Christ was an integral part of his system, but its significance reflects the new interests of the day. The economic and political transformation had proceeded far enough to become constructive in Edwards' thought. Though not fully developed, this new pattern had within it germs that the more revolutionary thought of the second half of the eighteenth century and the early part of the nineteenth century was to emphasize and carry into what seemed to a thorough-going Calvinist dangerous conclusions.

The influence of the rising economic interests of the day is seen in Edwards' discussion of sin as a debt which Jesus paid. In a way this is a conventional treatment, but as Edwards describes it, it is more economic than feudal. Here he differs from Anselm.[4] Jesus purchased redemption by his obedience and virtues, his death and resurrection.[5] Yet sin is itself not consist-

[3] Jonathan Edwards was born October 5, 1703, and died March 22, 1758.

[4] This conception runs throughout his treatise on the work of redemption, *Works* I, 297-516.

[5] *Works* I, 404 *seq.*

ently discussed as a debt.[6] The work of redemption accomplished by Christ is one phase of the total plan of God. Here Edwards' thought echoes Augustine's *City of God.* All history is a part of a plan culminating in the work of Jesus, and the death of Jesus is less prominent than his preëminence as the establisher of God's kingdom. Christ came into the world to purchase redemption, becoming incarnate and putting himself in a capacity for working out that redemption. Here he carries forward a complex of Protestant thought, for Jesus pays the price which pays our debt and "satisfies." By its intrinsic value and by the agreement between the Father and the Son it procures a title to us for happiness, and so it "merits." The satisfaction of Christ is to free us from misery and the merit of Christ is to purchase happiness for us. The satisfaction of Christ consists in answering the demands of a law which were consequent on the breach of the law. These were answered by suffering the penalty of the law. The merit of Christ consisted in what he did to answer the demands of the law which were prior to man's breach of the law, or to fulfill what the law demanded before man sinned, which was obedience.[7]

But although the economic and political patterns

[6] In his discussion of original sin, *Works* II, 310-510, Edwards is mostly concerned with the psychological rather then the economic or forensic pattern. Propensity, depravity, corruption, rather than debt, are his central words. In his discussion of redemption Edwards combines the economic with the psychological element.

[7] *Works,* I, 396, 401, 402.

are combined if not confused, it is really the political conceptions that dominated the thought of Edwards. As a defender of orthodoxy, he is unconscious of any difficulty with the sovereignty pattern. "Nothing is more agreeable," he says, "to the common sense of mankind, than that sins committed against anyone must be heinous proportionably to the dignity of the being offended and abused."[8] "The common sense of mankind" as an unquestioned axiom runs throughout the entire thought of Edwards. Man's relations with God are those of a debtor-subject liable to punishment, incapable of escaping guilt. "Justice requires that sin be punished because sin deserves punishment.[9] No repentance suffices to remove guilt, "for it belongs to God as the supreme Ruler of the universality of things to maintain honor and decorum in His kingdom." Yet Edwards follows Grotius in urging that "if God has given a law to his creatures that law must have sanctions . . . otherwise it fails of having the nature of law and is only of the nature of counsel or advice, or rather of a request."[10] The death of Christ is a vindication of this law. As the sufferings of a patron may

[8] *Works* IV, 228. See also the argument over the majesty of God, IV, 255.

[9] *Works* I, 582-85. See the sermon on God's sovereignty, *Works* IV, 548 *seq.*, especially 551, where the honor of God's majesty is made a premise or argument. For a full discussion of the sovereignty of God, see *Works* II, 144 *seq.*, and of men as enemies of God, IV, Sermons III. The Bible is a revelation "of God's design in the government of the world," *Works* I, 512. The moral government of God is discussed at length, *Works* I, 565-82.

[10] *Works* I, 587.

be the substitute for his client[11] the sufferings of Christ as the patron for his clients were more than those of the lost in hell, for he was really of the nature of man. The honor of God's majesty must be maintained and Christ suffered the "full punishment of sin that was imputed to him." [12]

In this thought of Edwards there is the same unquestioned acceptance of the political pattern which had marked prior Christian theology. His son, Jonathan Edwards, Jr., stated: [13] "As we have no other way to form an idea of God but to ascribe to Him in an infinite degree, all the perfections of a human spirit, abstracting all imperfections; so we have no way to form an idea of the divine government, but by ascribing to it everything most excellent in human government, abstracting all imperfections." But political idealism was moving from the emphasis of statute to that of abstract majesty or sovereignty. The decrees of God were still important for constructive thinking, but the general concept of sovereignty is more vigorously used; in fact, it lies beneath Edwards' view both of decrees and of predestination. It determines the conception of the need that sin should be punished by death in a judicial sentence "which God pronounced with regard to Adam's posterity, acting the part of the Judge." For God was

[11] This analogy is treated at length in *Works* I, 595-601.
[12] *Works* I, 607.
[13] *Works of Jonathan Edwards, A.M.,* 1865, vol. I, 501. This discussion of the atonement from which this quotation is taken shows how thoroughly political his theology was.

under obligation to punish, else law itself would "give place to rebellion of the sinner."

In some respects this position of Edwards resembles that of Grotius, and it was to be developed in the New England theology into a thoroughly Grotian conception. This fact itself is significant as indicating how, in a period of reflection a pattern tends to lose its sharply dramatic quality. It is one thing to speak of Jesus as actually bearing the punishment which otherwise would have been borne by others, and another thing to regard his sufferings as penal in the sense that they are of a sort to be regarded by God as vindicating his sovereign majesty. Change in the pattern accounts for the change in the conception of the atonement.

The two generations following the death of Edwards were filled with fierce theological controversy, but were uniformly unconscious of the fact that the real basis of much of the discussion was the attempt to interpret God's relationship to men under the categories of sovereignty, especially as regards the relation of man's responsibility to the doctrine of decrees. Every doctrine of the atonement which was set forth by the Calvinist theologians, especially in America, was concerned with the bearing of the death of Christ upon God and his sovereignty. But this was really a corollary of the general doctrine of God from which most of the theological difficulties emerged. The disputants are controlled by different conceptions of the state and so of the divine sovereignty. One sees in Hopkins the projection of the newer political attitude in the value given the death of Christ. He frankly admits what is implicit in all the Calvinist thought, an atonement so exclusively forensic as not to affect the moral condition of mankind. It is still under the power of sin. But the work of Jesus went beyond the satisfaction rendered by his death and suffering, for by his active obedience he honored the law and so obtained positive favor which those who accepted him as their feudal head could share. The atonement was sufficient to expiate for the sins of the whole world, but only those who believe and have faith in Jesus can be saved.[14]

III

Later literature dealing with the death of Christ has been more or less a phase of romantic theology, that is to say, in so far as there has been any effort to produce a doctrine of the atonement in accordance with the modern ways of thought, various writers have modified and have not abandoned the pattern of orthodoxy. They still say that men have such a sense of guilt before God as to fill them with despair as they think of the future. Even when the idea of punishment is somewhat replaced by the thought of outcome, the judicial and political presuppositions are unconsciously held. Yet in one particular the more recent writing is agreed. The idea of transfer of punishment from humanity to Christ is abandoned. The substitutionary

[14] Foster, *A History of New England Theology*, chs. 6 and 7.

atonement is too far away from our modern penology. But there is a deeper reason for this fact. There is an increasing tendency to abandon the conception of any punishment for sin and to substitute the conception of suffering that results from sin.

But in such a modification of the inherited doctrine the writers seem not to realize that they are combining two elements very difficult to reconcile, namely, the thought of man's relationship to God as that of a citizen or criminal, and the thought of outcome as involved in human activity. From the point of view of law a punishment is not something involved in the crime, but some form of suffering or loss imposed by authority upon the criminal. It is easily conceivable that one person could be substituted for another in the suffering of punishment without affecting the punishment. The father who had said he would whip the child who ate unripe fruit might consent to whip the elder son who saw the disobedient younger son suffering from indigestion, but he could not transfer the indigestion. Nor could that pain be coördinated with any conception of guilt. The two ways of thinking are two irreconcilable patterns. One can think consistently with either but not with both. It is the failure to recognize the impossibility of combining patterns that vitiates most modern treatments of the atonement and the work of Christ. The orthodox theory was consistent and had vigor. This romanticized orthodoxy has no convincing power for those who realize that the real relationship of man and God cannot be subsumed under the patterns of the state. What is needed is a frank realization of this fact and an abandonment of that type of liberalism that emotionally manipulates orthodoxy into a semblance of modern thought without abandoning the pattern which is its very heart. If men are to use the pattern of the state as that in which the relations of men and God are to be organized, then let them carry the figure through consistently in terms of guilt, punishment, and the absolute monarchy. But if, as is to be hoped, they come to realize that such a pattern is incapable of expressing the actual relationship of man to a cosmic God, they must seek a new pattern in which the death of Christ will be interpreted without reference to political and juridical practices.

IV

Nor is there much to be derived from identifying moral influence with the atonement. According to this view the death of Christ had no influence on God, but served as incitement to man to trust the love of God and to emulate the Master in sacrificial devotion to the pursuit of duty. This view is at least as old as Abelard and obviously has its value, but it seems to evade the issue faced by those doctrines of the atonement which have been given standing in the systems of theology. For while it is true that the death of Jesus exemplifies his loyalty to ideals and his recognition of the individual's participation in the life of the group to which he belongs, it leaves the reflecting mind in even deeper perplexity. For does not Jesus in becoming a mere fellow-victim of the world in which we ourselves live make the tragedy of life even more unintelligible? What sort of universe and what sort of moral order must that be in which a soul like Jesus should be only the victim of enmities and hatred? If such virtues as he represented are impotent, what hope is there for the average man and woman? However far the governmental interpretations of the death of Christ may be from our current way of thought, they at least did not leave Jesus in the status of fellow-victim, or the believer in any doubt as to the final triumph of love. It is pure dogmatism to say that without certain theological presuppositions the death of Jesus is calculated to stir men to repentance. If it be true, as Bushnell would argue [15] that the death of Jesus exhibits the love of God, such a revelation is possible only on the basis of an incarnation. Nor is it clear why love is displayed in God's participation in human sufferings. Might it not much better have been displayed in some revelation of the way to overcome suffering? The only reply seems to be that of a conception of the relation of men and God which no longer uses the old pattern of guilty subjects and guilty children.

V

In various other views of orthodox theologians who

[15] Bushnell, *Vicarious Sacrifice.*

wish to avoid the thorough-going logical exposition of their own systems, the death of Christ takes on a variety of values. Some of them, although satisfying earnest souls, on critical analysis appear little more than pious rhetoric. To say that the death of Christ shows God's conception of the awfulness of sin can hardly be taken as a scientific formula. Of course the death of Christ shows how men who were trying to be good as well as those who are without moral enthusiasms are driven to desperate and cruel acts, but the death of Christ was not necessary to make that revelation. Humanity knew it only too well. To say that God, by the death of Christ wished to reduce sin to its lowest terms so that it could be endured by Christ in a sort of inclusive vicarious act seems playing with words. What theologian knows so accurately what God thinks as to enable him to build a substantial doctrine upon his knowledge?

Even farther from philosophical worth seems the theory that Jesus so loved humanity and so identified himself with its sin and guilt that he repented for humanity and died literally of a broken heart. To one who is endeavoring to think in terms of reality it seems incredible that anyone should seriously put forth such a view as an explanation of the reason that Christ died or how he died. If one is to substitute rhetoric for facts it would be much better to recur to the allegorizing of Origen and the Alexandrians.

The fact is that all of the attempts at softening the political doctrine in which the death of Christ is interpreted ultimately fail to do that which the pattern itself did. There is no satisfaction in finding Jesus in the crowd of those who welcome Childe Rolande to the dark tower and inevitable defeat. The real power of the Christian doctrine of the atonement has always been that the death of Christ has had a share in adjusting the relations of men and God so that hope takes the place of discouragement and confidence the place of anxiety. All of these romanticizing theories have beneath them the suppressed premise that the relationship of man and God can be expressed in terms of disobedience and guilt. That is to say, they do not have any definitely new pattern. They differ only in the clarity with which the presupposition is recognized. Therein lies their inefficiency to do more than to soften the theology already possessed. The man in the street, like the scholar in his study, admires courage and believes he ought to possess self-sacrifice, but unless the death of Christ has more value than the expression of such a conviction, it is not likely to possess intellectual appeal.

The history of recent theological thought shows clearly that if one is to hold a pattern he should hold it courageously and systematically. If the results of such straightforward thinking are unacceptable he should find a new pattern. New truth can be put into old patterns no more than new wine into old goatskins.

CHAPTER XI

THE FUNCTIONAL VALUE OF THE DOCTRINES OF THE ATONEMENT

CHRISTIANITY has not been built upon pity for a suffering God or a defeated man. Christian orthodoxy has never sentimentalized the death of its founder. He was more than a martyr. The death of Lincoln gave new dignity to his whole life and silenced as bitter criticism as any to which a statesman was ever subjected, but it did not become an element in the reconstruction of the Union. The assassination of William McKinley doubtless stimulated interest in the extension of civil service, but it did not become a part of political theory or organization. Any account of the Christian religion must recognize that the death of Jesus has had a different value. It has become an element of the religion itself. Before it is classified with that of prophets like Isaiah and philosophers like Socrates or political ecclesiasts like Cranmer, inquiry must first be made as to just what function it has really had in the development of the Christian thought.

In brief, each exposition of the significance of the death of Christ has served the same function. It has endeavored not only to set forth God's saving, forgiving love, but also to meet objections against his moral right to forgive springing from contemporary practices. How true this is appears as we summarize the function of each doctrine of the atonement which has had its period of supremacy.

I

The theological meaning of the death of Christ has never been erected into any dogma like those contained in the Nicene and Caledonian creeds. It has never been standardized, and to this day it is susceptible of a number of interpretations. But this is not to say that these interpretations are functionally different. Whoever sees in Christianity a developing religion conditioned by and expressing social forces, finds in the doctrines of the atonement the expression of a permanent value vastly greater than the patterns in which it has been expressed. For all these doctrines spring from and variously express the desire to make clear that God's forgiveness does not contravene his moral order.

Christians consciously have a new life through faith in Jesus, who had been crucified and had been raised from the dead. If conscious of salvation, they may be assured of forgiveness—the conclusion which Paul so urgently argued in Galatians and Romans. But when one thinks of forgiveness he at once recalls preconditions of forgiveness in social practice. Not only that, but he begins to query whether those preconditions have been met in the forgiveness of God which he enjoys.

Unless they have been met, such forgiveness must appear morally unjustifiable. Each and every doctrine of the atonement is an answer to the need of such moral justification of God's gracious act.

The doctrines of the atonement thus spring from and express Christian experience as interpreted by successive social minds. Customs followed in the forgiveness of injuries are extended to God's action. He, like kings and common men, finds therein the conditions which make forgiveness moral. God's pardon, like men's, is justified by conforming to those social presuppositions which insure the maintenance of rights, law, honor, or sovereignty. God is conceived of as forgiving in accordance with socially approved practices. This makes his action morally acceptable to those who recognize the legitimacy of such conditions.

II

1. The New Testament exposition of the death of Christ illustrates this fact. The Christians were conscious of having received a new life in Christ. This they argued must indicate forgiveness, or in messianic terms, acquittal at the coming judgment. Here was a reconciliation with the deity which at first glance ran counter to the universal conditions of obtaining reconciliation. Jesus had justified belief in God's readiness to forgive by pleading the parental analogy. But this analogy failed to satisfy his disciples. Recourse was made to other customs. Among both Jews and Greeks

God's forgiveness was conditioned upon sacrifice. This sacrificial gift was accepted by the priest in the name of the god. The reconciliation was regarded as complete. This social practice was so universal as to determine the exposition of forgiveness on the part of God and its basis. There must have been a sacrifice. The Jewish Christians at first insisted that such sacrifices as were provided by the Mosaic Code should be offered. Paul's reply was that Christ was the Passover. Thus from a social practice there was drawn an analogy which helped Christians to make intellectually acceptable the grace of God which had already been shed abroad in their hearts. The preconditions of confidence in divine forgiveness had been met.

2. Beyond this interpretation of the death of Christ as satisfying the requirements of divine forgiveness set by current customs of worship, and as fulfilling prophecies, the early interpretation of the death of Christ made use of other social practices but above all that of releasing captives through payment of a ransom. The New Testament had spoken of Christ's death as a ransom. It never says to whom the ransom was to be paid, nor is a fair interpretation of the various references to ransom likely to show anything more than the high cost of doing a great service to someone else. But when the preacher appeared and effort was made to give something like practical bearing to the death of Christ beyond the allusion to it as sacrifice, the figure of ransom at once attracted attention. It is a military

practice with which all the ancient world was familiar. The captive was held by his captor until ransomed. Here lay an explanation of the death of Christ. In some mysterious way God recognized that Satan had control of pre-Christian believers in the underworld. Christ died that he might give his life as a ransom to Satan for these incarcerated worthies, and then broke away because of his divine power. Christ's death as a ransom to Satan helped the church to justify the church's confidence in divine forgiveness of the dead as well as of the living.

3. But sooner or later it was bound to lose its power, as Christian thinking passed over from the consideration of salvation as the giving of immortality to the judicial conception born of Latin Christianity. From the day of Augustine onward, transactions of the state were read into religion, both in the organization and administration of the church, and in the doctrines which were enunciated by the church. In the same proportion as new judicial and political ideas developed did Christian doctrines need new defense. These doctrines had accumulated as means of protecting the Christian faith, but had of themselves become identified with that faith. Practices of the church served as a stabilizing and even dominant defense of many of these doctrines, for men always hold tenaciously ideas which lie back of customs. The transformation of the dogmas into church life, rites, creeds, and customs, served to protect the faith as delivered to the twelfth century by the

past, but they did not meet objections raised by those who were outside the Christian community. To commend to them the incarnation, one could not appeal to the Bible, but must find something in the incarnation itself capable of meeting the objections to it. It was just this which Anselm set forth in his *Cur Deus Homo.* Again the argument is an extension of social practice as a means of understanding the relations between God and man. The explanation Anselm finds in the conditions demanded by forgiveness. He assumes the unquestioned view of feudal society that injury to one's honor demands satisfaction. This satisfaction in the case of God would be that of an infinite honor. Without it forgiveness was impossible. It required a man given infinite value to make such satisfaction, since man who had done the injury alone could render it. Therefore the Son of God became a man, so to suffer that it would be permissible for him to forgive sinners.

It will be noticed that this inhibition to forgiveness seems not to have been recognized by a civilization which was not feudal. The difficulty which feudal society saw in human forgiveness they read into divine forgiveness. The requirements by which the difficulty of forgiveness is resolved in social practice is raised as a presupposition into a doctrinal explanation of the right of God to forgive. Love is thus seen to meet the requirements of what was unquestioned morality.

4. When the national replaced the feudal order, the power of punishing became almost the essence of

the new monarchy. Sovereign right had to be maintained by the enforcement of the sovereign's law. The legitimacy of a king's government was deemed in proportion to his ability to punish those who refused to respond to the royal law as dispensed by the king's judges and enforced by the king's officers. There was always danger lest pardon should argue fear of one's administration. The king might be merciful, but he had to be just. The days of the arbitrary personal rule of oriental monarchs was replaced by statutory control, enforced by fear.

It is easy to see how this social attitude extended itself to the idea of divine administration. God was supreme sovereign; he maintained his authority by punishment. The world was rebellious and the world was under his displeasure. If he elected some to enjoy his favor and forgave them their share in universal rebellion, it was because the punishment due them had been inflicted on their representatives. God, like the king, could be merciful, but he was compelled to be just, that is, punitive. His punitive justice as well as his honor had to be satisfied. The only hope which any member of a condemned race could have under a sovereign capable of administering punishment was that his punishment had fallen on one capable of satisfying a sovereign God's obligation to punish every infraction of his law. That this punishment fell on an innocent person did not weaken its effect. Divine punishment had followed human disobedience; God's punitive justice was satisfied; he was free to forgive those whose punishment had been borne by Christ. Thus the substitutionary doctrine came to a world which could not believe that free pardon was compatible with justice. It is to be borne in mind that the underlying motive was not to find a way in which God might forgive, for there never was any question as to his forgiveness of those who had faith. The real difficulty was how to make plain to minds obsessed with the punitive obligation of a sovereign that the divine sovereign had a moral right to pardon. And such a difficulty the reformation doctrine of the atonement met and continues to meet where men still think of God under the rubrics of sixteenth-century monarchy.

5. In the eighteenth century the *bourgeois* class sought to replevy natural rights. Their success was also a triumph of commercialism. These two elements of a creative social mind set up their own qualifications for every sort of forgiveness. A debt, whether of rights or money, had to be paid. Until this was done a debtor was at the mercy of his creditor. The debt could be paid only by the actual transfer of assets. If the debtor himself could pay, he became free from the debt. If he could not, someone else could pay if he were able and disposed. From the middle of the seventeenth century, theology became unconsciously commercialized. Obedience became a debt, and good deeds in excess of obligations became transferable merit. The need of something in Protestant thought to

offset the effective penitential system of Rome contributed to this commercialization. In the original Reformation movement faith had been counted for righteousness; in the course of time it was the righteousness of Christ that was so counted. The relations of man to God were expressed in terms of debtor and creditor. Justification became a kind of bookkeeping. The merits of Christ were transferred to the sinner, and what was lacking in the sinner's righteousness was thus supplemented. The possibility that God could forgive a sinner depended upon the existence of that which could be transferred to the sinner's credit. The theologians easily found the death of Christ not only substitutionary and sacrificial, but his righteousness and merits were transferable to men. Thus again the grace of God in the act of forgiveness was deemed to be vindicated ethically. He was free not to punish the sinner because the sinner's debt had been paid. The methods of the court and of the accounting room suggested and removed moral objections to God's right to pardon.

IV

If one asks just what the permanent value in these various theories of the doctrine of the atonement may be, he is asking what function they have had in satisfying human need of successive periods. In answering such a question we follow the method already indicated. Any doctrine of the atonement is a social pattern which, submitted to historical examination, is seen to be an analogy intended to express the relations of God and man in the accomplishment of man's triumph over the physical and moral forces which otherwise would cause him suffering. They belong not to the field of experience but serve to rationalize experience. As a historical fact the death of Christ has no part in that actual transformation which the message of Christianity promises to its followers. The central thought throughout the entire course of the Christian movement has not been that of the death of Christ but that of the influence of God upon the human individual. The entire apparatus of Christian liturgy, sacrament, and worship, the doctrines of the incarnation, with the virgin birth and the modern dogma of the immaculate conception, regeneration through baptism, appropriation of the body and blood of Christ through the Eucharist, the obtaining and enjoyment of divine grace through all the sacraments, the doctrines of regeneration, sanctification, and the resurrection of the body, embody this central conception of transformation through a relationship with God, through faith in Jesus, a transformation which would not be possible without a God. In all of this system the death of Christ is not essential but contributory. It helps to solve the difficulty and tension which such experience and beliefs induce when the Christian salvation has been subsumed under social patterns. Had the ways of religious thought born of economic, political, and cult conditions been different, the value given to the death of Jesus would have been different.

It would certainly have played a part in the exposition of the content of the Christian religion, but the tension it would have resolved would not have been suggested by the organization of a state.

The facts being as they were, we seek to know just what needs and tensions of the religious life and thought these various doctrines met. In general they may be said to be those which on the plane of political life were caused and met by those institutions and practices utilized as patterns in the doctrines of the atonement. As the political elements operated in the actual social life of the community, so they functioned analogically in the doctrines. Even the pattern of sacrifice is at present no exception to the basic political and juridical interpretation of the death of Jesus. As a purely ritual act such sacrifice can have no meaning except to those who are under the domination of religious customs in which the altar with its sacrifices is literally demanded; that is to say, those whose religious thought is controlled by the practices of the Hebrew religion given typical value through a method of treatment of the scriptures. But to-day such an interpretation of the death of Jesus is seldom divorced from the political pattern. As a sacrifice he is said not only to have expiated for man's sins, but to have satisfied divine dignity or justice. It is the political pattern that actually gives value to the sacrificial.

In evaluating this pattern as it appears in the imperial, the feudal, and the national periods, there is little difficulty in discovering its elements and functions.

1. God's sovereignty, in which is expressed the conviction basic in all religion, that as the citizen is dependent upon and controlled by his emperor or king or feudal lord, so humanity is dependent upon God as a conditioning and controlling factor of his life.

2. Guilt. As the disobedience of a subject or vassal makes him liable to punishment by his superiors, so the maladjustment of a human being to God must result in suffering.

3. Divine pardon and forgiveness. As such an act on the part of a sovereign is conditioned by the repentance and plea of the offender but is wholly within the prerogative of the sovereign, so the forgiveness and pardon of God involve repentance on the part of humanity but is wholly the prerogative of God himself.

4. Satisfaction of honor or justice. As acts of pardon on the part of the sovereign must be consistent with his own sovereignty and without damage to that sovereignty or the law in which it is expressed, so the exercise of pardon by God must not violate his own sovereign position. Obviously the content of that sovereignty was set by political conditions prior to the rise of constitutional monarchy and democracy. As there must be a justification for the pardon of the sovereign other than his own will, so the death of Christ furnishes an appreciable means of meeting these conditions on the part of God.

Thus analyzed, the analogies which constitute the doctrines of the atonement are obviously coefficients of the social minds of different periods. They are attempts to show that the pardon given by God is consistent with moral ideals.

But this is by no means the last word to be said from the point of view of social psychology. That which the analogies set forth itself seems to be of the nature of analogy. The ultimate question is not how God pardons but whether there is anything in our actual experience with cosmic forces which can properly be described as pardon. For pardon itself is an element of the political pattern. So, too, is forgiveness—a less political concept, but one, nevertheless, which involves a distinctly anthropomorphic conception of God. The final question must be, What are the realities which these basic patterns themselves represent? The answer to this question will involve a new pattern consistent with to-day's creative social mind.

CHAPTER XII

THE DEATH OF CHRIST IN THE PATTERN OF PROCESS

It is one thing to organize a philosophy of religion and another thing to share in a religious movement like that of Christianity. In the former case one is at liberty to adopt such methods and forms of thought as may seem best. In the second instance one asks how far he can accept the values and loyalties which the movement has preserved in its customs and doctrines. If such an alternative were determined by the necessity of accepting uncritically the rites and doctrines of historical Christianity, intelligent people would very likely choose the philosophy of religion to the religion itself. And this would be particularly true in the case of the doctrine of the atonement. As I trust has appeared, the patterns used by orthodox doctrines of the atonement have lost their efficiency, nor can they be reinstated by any play upon words which makes atonement into at-one-ment. Yet for one who is historically minded this is by no means the end of the matter. Whoever feels sufficient confidence in the Christian movement as to wish to share in its continued service must treat it as he must treat all social processes. Christianity is concrete and not abstract; social rather than philosophical; organizing loyalties rather than metaphysics; a movement rather than a system. Above all, it furnishes moral motive by its perpetuation of values in a continuous group-life and by its method of energizing human life by contact with divine forces. To identify it with a doctrine or even with all the doctrines men have formed is to identify the whole with a part.

If one is to have any part in the Christian religion he must conserve rather than destroy its values. He joins a religious movement rather than a theology.

I

Considered historically, the Christian religion without the values expressed in a belief in a God-man expiating human sin and satisfying divine dignity and justice by his obedience and death, whose righteousness and obedience can be imputed to others at a day of judgment would certainly be different from the Christianity of the churches, whether Catholic or Protestant. It would not be so different in these particulars from the church of New Testament times, but it would differ from primitive Christianity in other elements. It could hardly be imagined that persons who have broken with current Christianity to the extent of giving up the orthodox doctrine of the atonement would believe that Jesus had gone in a discernible body to a heaven located above Palestine, or that he would ever come back through the sky with an angel blowing a trumpet to call the dead from an underworld. Whether such persons could be called Christians depends wholly upon the definition given the word *Christian.* If the history of Christianity shows anything, it is that the word has always been relative, a term describing membership in an organization perpetuating identical loyalties and attitudes far more than doctrinal patterns. A Christian of one age has always believed more or less than the Christian of another, and what is more, contemporary bodies of Christians have always differed among themselves. Primitive and Pauline, orthodox and heretics, Eastern and Western, Roman Catholic and Protestant, innumerable varieties of Protestants—what sort of definition can cover this variety of belief and practice? To generalize a definition of the Christianity given by one group would be inaccurate in the case of another.[1] What fellowship had the decrees of the Council of Trent and the papal Syllabus of Errors with the Saxon Visitation articles or the Baptist New

[1] Neglect of these historic differences in the term *Christianity* underlies all arguments of orthodox Protestant theologians. Inheriting, as they do, a succession of views which have been successively developed in the course of centuries, they find them all in the Bible. In a Bible which is infallible they find rites, views and theologies that were not thought of until centuries after the Bible was developed. See Machen, *Christianity and Liberalism.* The Roman Catholic Church, with its recognition of progressive revelation through itself occupies a much more tenable position logically than does Protestantism, for if anything is plain, it is that the Christianity of the Protestant Confessions is derived in large measure from the Roman Catholic theology current in the sixteenth century, and this in turn was the outgrowth of an historical process in which creeds and the decisions of councils are discernible factors.

Hampshire confession? In fact, the only definition that can possibly be given to Christianity is that it is the religion professed by people who call themselves Christians. And in this is the creative center of Christianity, for it is a description of group loyalty to Jesus. However Christians have expanded or reduced customs, rites, doctrines preserved in the group to which they belong, they have been at one in supreme loyalty to Jesus Christ as they conceived him. Their definitions of him may vary, their use of his life and death may differ widely, but loyalty to him as Savior and to a group which has similar loyalties is the distinguishing attitude of the Christian.

As we have seen, interpretations placed by his followers upon Jesus have varied. It could hardly be otherwise. The duty of a savior is to save, but from what? In the first group of followers the salvation desired was national and ethnic. With the Greeks it was death, and in the Western civilization it has been guilt and punishment. But always Jesus has been the last resort of an otherwise hopeless world. Men who have trembled at the thought of God have looked to him for deliverance from their fears. But the intelligent man of today is threatened by none of these fears. He is conscious of new tensions as he seeks to be a Christian in his own world. He is living in a world of law, or if not law, at least a world of process, whose operations are capable of intelligible classification. The poles of uncertainty have shifted and for at least the present moment he asks whether there is any reality to which they can point. He knows no Invisible King.

Still another tension arises. As the Calvinist, with his belief in the absolute sovereignty of God, found himself organizing town meetings and democracy, so the modern man finds himself bringing his scientific interest into the field of society at large. His question is no longer whether individuals have rights, but whether they are capable of freedom. Human society has become so complicated as to threaten the worth of the individuals who produced it. The disregard of honesty, law, and human life itself, so prevalent in democracies, is a constant source of doubt as to whether human life has any value apart from the enormous machine in which it would seem that individuals are nothing more than cogs.

Thus to a serious thinker, the supreme issue in the field of religion and morals amounts to this: was Jesus correct? Can one think of any reason or beneficent purpose in the cosmic process, and is love rather than coercion a basis upon which to build human society and organize one's own individual life? [2] Any attempt

[2] Walter Lippmann, in his *Preface to Morals*, has raised this question from the point of view of the liberal who has lost confidence in orthodoxy, but finds no satisfaction in his sophisticated liberalism. Royce, *Problem of Christianity*, Eucken, *Can We Still Be Christians?* and James in all his philosophical writings, as well as Hocking, *Human Nature in Remaking,* have faced the same question and given the same type of positive answer. The negative position of men like Nietzsche and Bertrand Russell is due to an unwillingness to give weight to the facts and considerations which are involved in a complete inventory of human experience.

to answer such questions by modifying the thought of God as a literal sovereign and of man's relationship to the cosmos as political simply complicates the problem. If Christianity as a religious movement is to have standing in the courts of to-day's intellect it will have to find a pattern in which to rationalize its attitudes which is as axiomatic for the modern man of our day as the pattern of sovereignty was to the modern man of the sixteenth century. The doubts which rise from a distrust of a pattern cannot be laid by insistence upon that pattern.

The abandonment of divine sovereignty means the abandonment of the entire political pattern. Human guilt is the correlate of divine sovereignty and cannot survive its disappearance. And with the disappearance of sovereignty as a literal attribute of God and of guilt on the part of man, the need of satisfying the divine honor or punitive justice also disappears and the death of Christ no longer gets significance as expiation, satisfaction, or vicarious suffering.

Have we then lost the values they set forth or escaped the tensions which such patterns express?

II

The development of Christian thought as to the death of Christ has always been conditioned by a conception of God. However much the philosopher might talk about the infinity of God, and however the theologians might discuss his omnipresence, omniscience, and omnipotence, in the Christian message of salvation anthropomorphism of the political type has always reigned. The naïve descriptions of the ancient world have been given a quasi-philosophical respectability, but they have continued secondary in the pattern which is the center of orthodox theology, namely, God as a transcendentalized ruler. Orthodoxy is cast in the pattern of politics multiplied by infinity.

But such conceptions of God fail utterly to satisfy men who know that God is no more a king than he is an individual circumscribed by space and time. Our knowledge of the universe makes sovereignty as a pattern for the conception of human and divine relations futile. No small part of the confusion of to-day's religious and moral thought springs from this fact. The universe of the chemist and physicist and astronomer is too great for any sovereignty. The atom and the nebula do not suggest a king, nor is the relationship of men to the universe to be described as that of subjects to a monarch. Such a pattern is now seen to be the picture of poetry, not the statement of a fact.[3]

Any conception of God must be made as we make any definition, but in the nature of the case it must be frankly admitted to be a description rather than a definition of that which lies behind experience. In speaking of God we use our experience as in the forma-

[3] "We are living in a totally new world, and the knowledge of God must begin with a knowledge of the world-process as it is revealed daily in the fields of observational and experimental science." Simpson, *Nature, Cosmic, Human, and Divine*, p. 151.

tion of any other concept, and this will be inevitably poetic or symbolical. But do not even the scientists the same? What else, when they talk about atoms as if they had purpose and military ambitions?[4] One cannot read any scientific work without a feeling that in expressing the results of their experience of nature the scientists are forced to create a new mythology. There seems to be no way of understanding our world except as its scattered elements are brought into the order of some intellectual form born of experience. It is not until facts are so organized that they become really intelligible. And even then it is the experience of the scientists rather than stars and electrons themselves that are interpreted. In too many cases the absorption of scientists in minute experiments makes them indifferent to the organization of any reliable world-view and to the presence of human elements in the most mechanical experiment. But the multiplication of details is no more an understanding of the universe than the study of its punctuation marks is an understanding of *Hamlet*. We give unity to the universe only as we know it in the experience of the scientist.

When, therefore, we organize our conception of God by the use of our experience as persons, we are not outraging any intellectual respectability. We no more know gravitation and light than we know God. In both cases we interpret a force through our experience. Our chief obligation is to see that the pattern which

[4] Cf. Eddington, *The Nature of the Physical World*, ch. 1.

we use in our interpretation is itself reputable and in accordance with what we have discovered to be actual. That pattern for religion we find in our experience of the relation of an organism to its active environment and of individuals to groups.

If we once admit that human beings are the outcome of the cosmic process we can safely argue that there are forces within it which are capable of evolving them. Man is organic, not mechanistic [5] in the universe. Nor can this fact be swept away by any comparison between the fish and the ocean. The ocean did not produce the fish although it does minister to fish as an environing force. It is not a superfish, but it is a physical and chemical condition of a fish's life. And the fish must live within it according to chemical forces. But a fish has no personal value. A man must respond to other forces than the material. As we do not think that chemical and physical forces are any less operative in an environment to-day than they were before our world was evolved, so are we forced to believe that the personality-evolving elements of the universe are still operating as elements of the environment which conditions our life. We can no more be detached from them as they continue the timeless process than from light and heat. Religion is the attempt to utilize our experience as persons in setting up

[5] I use this word in its commonly accepted meaning. If used in the sense given it by Herrick, C. J. *The Thinking Machine*, it is not opposed to social and idealistic interpretations of human values.

relations with these personality-producing forces. That is to say, we act toward the process in the midst of which we are as we act toward the human environment in which we are. Experience in the latter becomes the pattern for adjustment of ourselves to the former. When, therefore, we find in those complicated mechanisms we call human bodies that which responds to rational and purposeful approach, we feel the same confidence in approaching the larger total activity from which we have emerged and with which we must live. We do not know exactly what the term personality means in either human or superhuman realities,[6] but we know that what we call a personal relation with the outer world is very different from what we call impersonal relations with that world. It is one thing to have a man a friend and another thing to treat him as if he were a mass of chemicals. And we know that we cannot set up these personal relations with that which does not respond personally. It is in this sense that we say "you" to some human body, meaning thereby that we discover in relationship to a physical mechanism something more than can be found by chemistry or physics or even biology, and with this we establish personal relations. That is, we treat a human being as like ourselves, rational, purposeful, and social.

This is the pattern which we can use in religion. The individual is in personal relation with those personality-

[6] Cf. Webb, *God and Personality*; Streeter, *God and the Struggle for Existence.*

evolving elements of an environing process as he is to society. Such a pattern, born of biology and sociology, lies outside discussion of immanence and transcendence. Were not the expression so paradoxical, it might almost be called a distributive monism, since the ultimate reality we can imagine or infer is activity from which we select personality-producing elements as distinct from others. For religious purposes it is enough to hold that human life is conditioned by a relationship to an eternally creative environment in the midst of which are continuing forces that have produced personality and with which relations can and must be set up which advance personality. To such elements of the environing Activity which demand and permit appropriation on the plane of personality and which can be seen in the intelligibility of all nature, we give the name God. He is the "You" of the cosmic process.

III

In so saying we do not personify the universe, and we are the farthest possible from pantheism. We are using a pattern and not a metaphysic. That pattern involves the participation of persons in society quite as truly as needs of the amœba and the flower in the crannied wall. Such relations are not static, but those of process in which there is observed change. The intercourse of persons is conducive to changes due to reciprocal influence and the relationship of man and God must be conceived of in a similar fashion. Mankind is not related to the cosmic processes as is a stone or a tree or even a living animal. He has gone farther in the process of coördination and sets up relationships with those elements of the total environment with which the sub-human existences can have no commerce. All the more complicated, therefore, is the question of his response to the environment. He is in a situation in which he must adjust himself to and appropriate an increasing number of elements, otherwise he will fail to go on with the process from which he has emerged. It will not be enough for him to control the impersonal forces like electricity and light; he must set up help-gaining relationships with those personal forces in the midst of which all the universe exists, but to which only persons can respond. In distinguishing between God and the process as a whole, we are no more creating a dualism than does the psychologist when he speaks of consciousness and brain. Humanity is of course concerned with its total cosmic environment, for it is conditioned by chemical and physical forces, but just as we set up relations with a human being on different levels —physical and personal—do we set up relations with a total environment on different levels. The capacity to make such cosmic adjustments on the level of personality and by the use of the experience born of dealing with other persons is the distinguishing mark of humanity.[1]

[1] See Boodin, *Cosmic Evolution*; Mathews, *The Contribution of Science to Religion*, chaps. 17, 18.

Such a pattern enables us to reëxpress those relations which the pre-scientific thought pictured in terms of sovereignty. That is to say, human life is conditioned by its dependence upon these personality-creating forces. However much men, in endeavoring to account for evolutionary changes may debate the relative importance of the organism and its environment, it is certain that forces which make the evolutionary process possible are antecedent to that which is evolved. Whether or not we call evolution emergent, it is at least coöperative. *B* does not evolve from *A* without appropriating something from the already existing environment. In the same way we must think of God as antecedent to man.

This fact enables one to reëxpress an essential element in all doctrines of the atonement: the initiation of the reconciliation between God and man came from the side of deity. It was God, men believed, who set Christ forth as a propitiatory gift. It was the second person of the Trinity, men believed, who paid the ransom to Satan and satisfied the divine honor and the divine justice. Without the prior doctrine of the incarnation every doctrine of the atonement would lose meaning. While in popular presentation it has often been true that the contrast is drawn sharply between Christ and God, from the point of view of an orthodox system of theology such a misinterpretation is forestalled by the doctrine of the Trinity. God is not placated by the death of Jesus, but God the Father finds it moral to forgive by virtue of the vicarious suffering of God the Son, who has become incarnate in humanity. While attempts at systematizing such a conception have seldom been philosophically consistent, functionally they have been at one. However expressed, the impotence of man has been offset by the initiative of God. No orthodox thinker has undertaken to say that God was made propitious by a human sacrifice. It has been the divine Son in the human Jesus that has made the reconciliation of man and God morally conceivable.

The unity between God and men has been cast in a pattern of sovereignty born of the political interpretation of the relation of men and God. Once grant that this cannot be taken literally, our effort should be to discover what values the pattern represents. As in the interpretation of all analogies the evaluation is to be gained by the establishment of a sort of proportion. As anything which made it legitimate for an absolute ruler to forgive a repentant but impotent rebel was to the act of forgiveness, so the death of Christ was to God in his relation to men. It is the comparison that is the truth in the pattern itself. Stripped of all its figurative interpretation, the fact remains that men who have been out of right relationship with God have been brought into such relationship with him through his coöperation. The progress of the organism is in the direction set by the process in which it is integrated. In the case of humanity this progress is toward increased personality.

When such a pattern is brought to the consideration of the Christian life its significance is at once apparent. The cry of Augustine that men were made for God and that they are restless until they find their rest in him is a statement of fact rather than a mere eruption of emotion. Until the organism is affected by some hitherto ineffective element of the environment it will remain unchanged. It does not progress with the process. This is to state in one set of terms that which the Christian teachers, like those of all developed religions, have emphasized, namely, that the triumph over the physical order and the development of proper morality are conditioned by coöperation with those personality-evolving forces to which we apply the term Deity. Men in such relation move toward freer personality. In the case of Christianity such experience is illustrated and epitomized in Jesus. His experience is revelatory of the divine coworking with humanity.

But the analogy is not only that of the organism in an environment but of the environment in the organism. As one can understand how air conditions life only by the study of living organisms, as one can fully understand social custom only as one studies its effect upon the individual, so we may say the operation of God in human life may be seen in the historical Jesus. This is, of course, another way of restating the old orthodox position of the councils that in Jesus is to be seen a person embodying and exhibiting both a human and a divine nature. Whatever one may feel about the permanence of the Nicene metaphysic, that which it sets forth can hardly be denied, viz., every man is subject to the modifying influences of those elements in the total activity in which he lives and moves and has his being, which have coöperated with other elements to produce the human personality. In a sense perhaps truer than is sometimes declared, man has shaped the idea of God in his own image, but, it should be added, only because God (as already defined), working in the prehuman complex of life, so recombined its elements as to make self-directive personality possible. Just as man has been conceived of as in the image of God, so do we reach a fully moral image of God through the study of experience like that of Jesus, and to a less degree one may add, in the spirit of orthodox trinitarianism, in the experience of all religious men. Good will as well as reason is in the cosmic process.

Such conclusions as these are inevitably challenged by the phenomena of human life. Too frequently we seem to be at the mercy of forces which are impersonal, which thrust upon us physical suffering, social disorder, and death. Is it possible to see in such phenomena the operation of that progress-causing God about whose love we speak so easily? Philosophies of all sorts have answered this question, some negatively and some hopefully. At all events we can see that suffering does not exist until something superior to the cause of suffering has been evolved. The Christian, however, has no doubt about the matter. In the experience of Jesus he constantly discovers the environing influence of a loving God. So Jesus himself estimated his life and so have countless men who have become his followers. But the supreme conviction of faith in this revelatory worth of his experience lies in the assertion that in his humiliation and death, the tragedy was no miscarriage of cosmic order or bare mischance. For he overcame. His experience was a sample and illustration of that economy of process by which men under the influence of their personality-forming environment move forward to mastery of the physical and impersonal elements of themselves. Impersonal forces may crush them, but even as they are crushed they know themselves as persons superior to those forces.

Such a revelation is of course tragic and perplexing. Why should there be such a universe as ours? Were not the Gnostics right when they declared that the Creator was not the God whom Jesus revealed but rather a malignant demiurge?

The answer of Christianity to such a question has always been constant. God the Father is the maker of heaven and earth, but in the experience of Jesus He is set forth as coöperative good will. And in this experience, independent of a discarded metaphysics, is set forth that method of cosmic activity in the field of personality which we see in all other fields. Progress toward fuller assimilation of personality-producing forces involves the abandonment of that which is already accomplished. Man exchanges comfort for moral development and life itself for the life of the spirit. From such a point of view the death of Christ is not to be described as satisfaction of dignity or justice, but as an exponent of the forces inherent in the process through whose aid the loss of that which is good conditions the gain of that which is better—a personality more individual, less dependent upon its earlier stages and more appropriative of the personality-evolving activity of God.

IV

No human being is independent of the process through which personality has been and still is being developed. That is the truth in mechanistic interpretations of life. What then if men are not co-operatively responsive to such an environment? Can personality-evolving forces be ignored or opposed?

The answer is inevitable. The outcome is suffering. The Christian church has never cajoled men into believing in a good-natured deity. From the very start Christians have been at the mercy of a universe that brought suffering and a social order that refused even to the point of bloodshed to accept the ideals of the Christian religion. Western civilization owes an incalculable debt to those religious leaders who, however crude their formulas, refused to embrace the easy dualism that matter is bad and that only spirit is good. Again and again organized Christianity has repudiated some heresy that championed such teaching. As a result the Christian religion has put no moral interpretation on the world with which science deals. Its dogma has never insisted that matter was evil. But at the same time it has believed that suffering was attendant upon violation of whatever laws are to be found within the universe. Theologically such laws were interpreted as the will of God, which humanity had from the start violated and in consequence propagated a human nature "corrupt and guilty." When once we ask what was signified by the pattern in which men found original sin, the answer is immediate and almost surprising. It is the principle of atavism—the tendency of an organism no longer well adjusted to those elements of the environment which have made its present character possible to revert to lower forms which in its progress it has recapitulated. Sin can indeed be described as conscious yielding to the backward pull of outgrown good, a maladjustment to the personality-evolving forces of the environment in the midst of which we as persons must live. Concretely, it is anti-social and anti-personal behavior judged in its relation to the cosmic process.

But such maladjustment is only one reality of the biological-sociological equivalent of the guilt pattern. Guilt implies a fear of future vengeance on the part of the society whose will has been violated. In the forensic analogy so central in Protestantism this fear of divine punishment is the very opportunity of justification by faith. No analogy can accurately express the permanent values of the Christian religion which is indifferent to this consciousness of deliverance from liability to delayed divine punishment.

Stripped of analogy, this apprehension of punishment is seen to be the expectation of suffering because of maladjustment to the conditioning environment of process. The religious interpretation of nature can never omit the apprehension of delayed punishment, or in the new pattern, delayed resultant suffering. Such an apprehension is derived from social experience, and is inevitable in the pattern itself. Just as the apprehension of punishment in the case of the state led men to have a sense of guilt, that is, liability to delayed punishment, at the hands of God, so an understanding of the laws of life and of the danger of disregarding the laws of cosmic process finds reëxpression in the apprehension of the outcome of wrong relationship between man and God. The abandonment of the politico-judicial pattern may relieve one from the fear of an irresponsible sovereign God, but a sense of the inevitability of outcomes is not quieted. We know too much about suffering which comes from disturbed relationships with nature to be complacent if we think of such relations on the plane of personality. If opposition to the force which we call gravitation or to those chemical forces we call fire, or to those biological forces which lie within the cell brings suffering, it is impossible for the religious soul not to feel that living as if there were no coördinating reason in the process of the universe and no personal values in human society will similarly lead to suffering. And above all else, there is the fact of death, the supreme outcome of man's failure permanently to adjust himself to the physical and chemical universe in the midst of which he must live. To many minds death constitutes the final denial of love within the universe because it seems the absolutely unavoidable evil whose coming can at best only be postponed.

The breakdown of the orthodox conception of future punishment is complete. Only an illiterate mind can be terrorized by the fear of the devil and of hell which nerved Thomas à Kempis, Martin Luther, and Jonathan Edwards. For them sovereignty with its corollaries was an effective pattern. Hell was as vivid as a torture chamber of a feudal lord or a fire in a field of peat. Justification was as definite as the acquittal in a royal court. But the heaven and hell of the theologian have now no more standing in the minds of intelligent people than Sheol of the Hebrews and the Hades of Homer and Virgil. They expect no Day of Judgment or separation between the sheep and the goats. They participate in cosmic forces whose mysteries are being disclosed. In a universe of billions of stars and distances too great for measurement even by light years, the celestial geography of Paul and the New Testament is as unthinkable as that of Dante.

The vivid pictures of judgment and punishment for

sin, whether that of humanity or of the individual, do not originate, but dramatize this instinctive fear of suffering and of death because of maladjustment of the living organism to its environment. If religion is to utilize this pattern the significance of the death of Christ must be included within it. Maladjustment brings suffering to all those involved in it—the group as well as the individual. And Jesus was the innocent victim of such maladjustment.

V

If once we cease thinking of Jesus in the picturesque terms of earlier theological thought and ask just exactly what Jesus may be regarded as having done we find an answer in which his death is a definite element. And interestingly enough such a view is far closer to that of the New Testament itself than to later ecclesiastical teachings. Jesus' experience has value for us because he was subject to the conditions in which maladjustment to personality-developing forces causes suffering. And that maladjustment was both social and cosmic. It was social in that those among whom he lived were indifferent to the personal values of human life. It was cosmic because men ignored the creative process of love from which personal values emerge.

The older theologians were wise in joining the "active" obedience of Jesus with his "passive" obedience. For it is the totality of his experience that is significant as a way of salvation. In the life of every man there rises repeatedly the question whether one can control actions by ideals. If the gospels make anything plain it is that such a problem was always in Jesus' mind. From the point of view of his own ambition he was a failure. There were few that found the strait gate and the narrow way, and there were many that found the wide gate and the broad way. The rulers of his people refused to regard him except as a disturber of peace and ultimately political peace. He was without home or occupation, surrounded by a group of unimportant men, the very number of whom is a pathetic reminder of his failure to win the twelve tribes of Israel. The wise and the prudent had failed to see the meaning of his teaching, the babes had perceived it. And all the time there was projected across his mind the possibility of victory that might be his as the leader of a revolt and the founder of a kingdom. Yet Jesus remained true to his ideals. Swept along in the current of pre-revolutionary days, he paid the penalty of its leaders.

The tragedy of his execution is all the darker since he was a victim of religious idealism and political order. It is difficult to realize this, for we have become so accustomed to think of the Pharisees as hypocrites and the Romans as brutal that it is hard to see them as representatives of progress. Yet the Pharisees represented a serious attempt to bring men into accord with the will of God and the Romans enforced respect for administrative unity and public order. Their opposition to Jesus was anything but accidental. He and they represented antithetical approaches to the problems of life. On the one side were the will to command and the will to power, on the other side were the will to share and the will to serve. In actual experience these two opposites have progressively adjusted themselves to each other and the social process discloses a passage from customs and institutions built upon the one to customs and institutions built on the other. But Jesus was not historically minded. His thought was absolute rather than relative. He was not interested in the techniques of life but in its moral attitudes. Had he been a leader of a political party or of a social movement he would have been forced to develop some program by which the world as he saw it could be transformed into the world as he planned it. But he was neither of these and therefore all the more dangerous to those who were seeking to develop a better social order with the inherited techniques of contemporary religion and politics. A social order was confronted by the kingdom of God. What was socially good was threatened by that which was socially better, and the champions of the inherited good executed the champion of the future.

The death of Jesus not only makes clear the difference between the two worlds of thought but also shows how the spirit of coercion and acquisitiveness, even when expressed in the higher ranges of human needs, brings suffering. It is this fact which some of the modern theories of the atonement try to express, when the death of Christ is said to set forth the sinfulness of sin. What it really sets forth is how a society bent upon maintaining privileges brings suffering to such of its individual members as question the permanence of the *status quo.* The subjection of personal values to economic or political results in suffering because the social process is opposed to the personality-producing forces of the universe. For there can be no release from the causal sequence in the process of personal development any more than in that of the physical world. Men must establish a wider range of creative relationships than is possible for non-personal existences. One can no more live the good life by flouting the conditions set by the personal environment of society or the personality-evolving forces of the cosmic process than he can ascend by running down an escalator. In both cases his action is irrational and dangerous.

The love of which Jesus speaks and which his opponents slighted is the treatment of our human environment as if it were personal. That is his technique of adjustment to and appropriation of the process which carries men to newness of life. It is coördination on the plane of personality. God is on the side of fraternity. Jesus knew that such action would mean sacrifice on the part of those who adventured it, since it must always urge the abandonment of privileges sanctioned by a social order. But he had no interest in the sophisticated life that seeks the easiest way of adjustment to human circumstance. If his followers were not ready to take up their cross and follow him they should stay at home. If men were to be at one with their fellows, like their master, they must face a social order that would misunderstand and abuse them. Yet even in their enemies they were to find those they could love. Instead of coercing men into goodness they were to rely upon service. Fraternal relations with men are indispensable for filial relations with God.

Halfway measures did not appeal to Jesus. He did not with folded hands submit to fate, but until his voice was stilled in death he treated those about him as if they were persons rather than animals, and by appeal and denunciation sought to arouse within them the confidence in love on which his own life was based. For to him love was in the cosmic process. The God of nature was a Father.

In the willingness of Jesus to hold tenaciously to the supremacy of good will we find one significance of his death. He chose to die at the hands of a society he would show the true value of life rather than abandon his dependence upon the fatherliness of God and his practice of treating men as persons. The question which such a tragedy thrusts upon us is whether he died self-deceived or whether such loyalty to an interpretation of God and to good will among men is justifiable. If humanity has no value beyond the biological, which may in turn be chemical, the only reply can be that the death of Jesus was unnecessary. He might much better have remained an unknown carpenter in Nazareth. But if one believes that the human individual has other values, that by proper relation with personality-producing forces personality can be developed, and life ordered toward ends that are not already gained by the animal life from which humanity sprang, then the death of Jesus is the price by which he maintained something more valuable than his life.

Whatever the formula in which this exchange of living for life is expressed, Jesus is its central figure—a successful, revealing experiment in the adjustment of the human with those conditioning elements of the total environing process with which personal relations on our part are possible. The Christian religion has always seen in the life of Jesus the revelation of what is meant by "being at one with God." But the establishment of such a relationship on the part of maladjusted men does not need to be expressed in terms of forgiveness or pardon or justification. It can also be expressed in the language of biology and sociology. As one who was actually saved from the backward pull of outgrown goods, both social and physiological, because of a perfect relationship with the personality-evolving forces of the universe, Jesus becomes an exponent or revelation of the method of right relations with the personality-producing forces of the universe. He becomes a savior because he was himself saved. One can understand how legitimate was the insistence of the ancient church that Christ was truly flesh, that he truly died, and that he truly was raised from the dead. The very heart of Christianity as a religion of salvation centers around the conviction that such salvation is possible for humanity because Jesus himself was human. In his way of life is to be seen, therefore, the method by which men are to overcome their apprehension of the results of maladjustment to the creative forces of the universe by setting up new relations with forces which will assure the avoidance of the evil effects of the older and imperfect relations.

But all this would be impossible unless Jesus not only participated in the moral struggles of mankind, sharing in the results of human sin and error, but also submitted to death. For men want to be saved from death. Sometimes this desire is simply physical, to be free from dying; at other times it is the desire to be saved from the loss of individuality which death seems to threaten. If there is a way of so living in relationship to the creative personal forces that such loss can be avoided and individuality not only be saved but developed, he who announces it must also experience it. As he who would rescue men from drowning must enter the water, as one who would rescue buried miners must enter the mine, as those who discovered the way of preventing yellow-fever had to submit to the conditions which bring yellow-fever, so he who would save men from the effects of their yielding to the backward pull of outgrown good, from the suffering and death which are the outcome of maladjustment to forces which otherwise bring happiness and life, must himself submit to the conditions and show the validity of his method in his own experience.

From this point of view the death of Jesus is to be interpreted in the same spirit as that in which orthodox Christianity always has interpreted it—as something other than a misfortune and a tragedy, or even as an example of devotion to an ideal. It was an element in his work as savior. Whether described as a ransom or satisfaction or as an experimental test it has its value not in its tragedy but in its outcome. However it may hesitate to accept the empty tomb and a physical body of the risen Christ, to-day, as in the New Testament time, Christian thought cannot dissociate the death of Christ from those experiences his disciples described as his resurrection. He not only showed how by appropriating the influence of God and by the practice of love one can rise superior to temptations of all sorts, especially appeals to outgrown goods like force, but he also made men believe that by the same adjustment human life can be made superior to death. In both cases the outcome is due to a setting up of dynamic relations in which the individual is helped by the co-operation of the environing forces which develop personality itself. Not Good Friday but Easter is the true Holy Day of Christians. For it heralds the fact that Jesus, while suffering from others' maladjustment to personality-evolving forces of the cosmic process, triumphed through his own adjustment to those forces.

VI

It may be urged that this pattern drawn from the scientific conception of life lacks appeal. If so, it would probably be of little use in legitimatizing the Christian faith in the possibility of union with God on the part of those whose minds employ other patterns. But this is by no means to say that the effort to find a new pattern is unwarranted. What of those who cannot use the older patterns? Once men realize that all theology rationalizes religious experience only tentatively and functionally, they will be much more friendly toward those who claim the same loyalties but use different doctrinal formulas. It is only when one insists that a doctrine which is obviously analogical is to be accepted as literal that intolerance raises its head. And in any case the interpretation of the death of Christ is not a matter of religious experience, but of theological belief. Only as it gives men new confidence in the validity of their trust and hope of the possibility of union with God is it of any help. And if one believes that following the teaching and appropriating the attitude of Jesus will establish one in a new and transforming relationship with divine forces, he should be more concerned in bringing his life into line with such a belief than with precise formulas. For the Christian religion is not a doctrine of the atonement or of anything else, but a way to the attainment of the highest personal goods through personal relations with men and God. Any exposition of the death of Christ should aid the development of such a life. Only thus will it be consistent with the teaching and example of Jesus, whose gospel made love the sole way of approach to a God who himself was loving. Any interpretation of his death which detracts from moral incentive and leaves man without confidence in moral ideals or in the practicability of love as a basis of the social order, hinders the accomplishment of the end Jesus set himself to accomplish. It would be hard to think of anything more incongruous than an exposition of the death of Jesus that deadened that sense of moral responsibility which was the center of Jesus' own teaching.

The fact that he paid with his life for his loyalty to his estimate of human values and divine coöperation will deter no man who accepts Jesus as his ideal. Loyalty like his is the only escape from pessimism. The humanist who has forgotten the universe is as unconvincing as the mechanist who has forgotten humanity. Moral doubts must be satisfied and hope be restored on the plane in which they arise. We must not distrust humanity because it acts in a subhuman way. That precisely is the message of Jesus. The defeat which he endured was as nothing compared with his triumph over doubt and hatred, fear and death, through his integration with the personality-producing forces in the process in which humanity is involved. Only one who misunderstands him and the worth of human personality alike can think of his ethics as glorifying defeat or passive resistance. He would have his followers adventure rather than meditate. They must go on with the process toward the perfection of the Father. They must push out the frontier of morality until they treat all men as brothers, giving justice rather than seeking justice. That way, he said, was God's. And lest men might think that such appeal was the rhetoric of the lecture hall, he sealed his faith in the supremacy of love with his blood.

But his death was a result of others' maladjustment to the process rather than a "satisfaction," an exhibition of his confidence in the divine economy rather than a penalty of rebellious humanity. Fraternity in his sense of the word is born of a faith that to make men's personal worth the supreme good of human relations is the way by which men come into revivifying fellowship with the divine. And this coördination of the individual with man and the cosmic process on the level of personal value is a supreme message that he gave the world. He left his followers no catalog of duties, for duties are relative. He organized no program of social reform, for programs can never be final. He praised no contemplative quietism, for life must have its adventure. Through his experience men know God as through the experience of the scientist they know electrons. Only by living personally, that is, with the sacrificial social-mindedness of Jesus does one come into unity with men and God. The prayer that brings fellowship with God must, like his, embody the social attitude that makes men helpers of their kind. God forgives as men forgive. But the result of such coördination with human personality in the actual practice of fraternity is a life made more personal through the coöperation of the personal environment of God. This advance in personality because of a response to personal forces in humanity and in the cosmic process is in truth salvation. Like the experience of Jesus, it is a triumph over the backward pull of the outgrown goods of the physical life and of social history, through union with the God of process. In the light of such an outcome death is a negligible episode. Did not Jesus die?

INDEX

Abelard, on death of Christ, 110
Adam, disobedience of, corrupts human nature, 96; representative of the race, 133
Anselm, doctrine of the atonement, 106*sq.*
Arminianism, 140
Atonement, Paul, 50, 53; Irenæus, 84; Luther's doctrine of, 128; a pattern, 141; functional value of, 166, 173, 175; and morality, 204. See Death of Christ.
Augustine, influence of, 93, 95; influence on later theologies, 122

Baptism, laver of immortality, 82
Bourgeois period, religious movements of, 20
Butler, on the death of Christ, 149

Calvin, use of political pattern, 130*sq.*; on death of Christ, 123
Christianity, a phase of history, 10; a religion of salvation, 34; how developed, 40; mediæval tendencies, 114; defined, 178*sq.*; central thought of, 205
Covenant theology, 133*sq.*

Death of Christ, absence of teaching concerning by Jesus, 42-44; justified by prophecy, 45, 48; interpreted as a sacrifice, 50; interpreted by Paul, 67; interpreted by Irenæus, 84; as a satisfaction of the dignity of God, 106*sq.*; interpreted by Abelard, 110; as a satisfaction of the punitive justice of God, 123; as an example of love, 161, 162; as a part of his saving work in process, 191*sq.*, 203; due to wrongdoing of others, 199
Deism, 144
Democracy, effects on theology, 152
Dignity of God, 106*sq.*
Doctrines, social origin of, 11, 15*sq.*, 23-26

Edwards, Jonathan, on the death of Christ, 153-57
Eucharist, development of, 56-60; bread of immortality, 82

Faith, in Luther and Calvin, 125
Feudalism, 16; pattern of the atonement, 103*sq.*

Gnosticism, influence of, on Paul's thoughts, 68-71
God, conception of, 182-87
Græco-Roman world, character of, 17*sq.*; doctrines originating in, 19, 21
Gregory of Nyssa, on the death of Christ, 87
Grotius, on the death of Christ, 137*sq.*
Guilt, real meaning of, 194-98

Human nature, theized, 80

Imperialism as a doctrinal pattern, 92
Irenæus, on the death of Christ, 84

Jesus, as savior, 37, 38; death of, in theology, 38; reality of human nature of, 81; preaches to the dead, 83; imputed righteousness of, 130, 133
Justification by faith, formal concept, 61

Locke, on the death of Christ, 146
Luther, doctrine of atonement, 128

Mass, as a sacrifice, 57
Messiah, conquest of Satan by, 41
Mystery religion, Paul's use of, 71-73

Nationalism, rise of, 19

Orthodoxy, efficiency of, 159; permanent values in its doctrine of the death of Christ, 205

Pattern, defined, 31; compared with analogies, 32*sq.*; messianic, 44*sq.*; sacrifice, 50-54; monarchy, 119-21; process, 184*sq.*
Paul, on death of Christ, 50, 53
Politics, pattern for doctrines, 21*sq.*, 89*sq.*; modification of, 158
Punitive justice, satisfied by death of Christ, 123

Ransom to Satan, 86
Recapitulation, 84
Reformation, nature of, 117*sq.*

Sacrifice, death of Christ as, in Paul, 50, 53; in Hebrews, 53, 54; partaken of by Christians, 56, 57; justification, 77
Salvation, different views of, 34-36; from death, 62, 74; a transformation of personality, 62-65, 80
Satan, control of the dead, 85; ransom to, 86
Socinus, on the death of Christ, 136
Sonship, 79*sq.*
Sovereignty as a doctrinal pattern in Calvin, 130*sq.*

Theology, functional nature of, 14, 26-29; not philosophy, 20